"Who you follow wil
journey will look like.
uncomplicated it is to ...

Bob Goff, author of *New York Times* bestsellers *Love Does*,
Everybody Always, *Dream Big*, and *Undistracted*

"If you are looking for a book to put in the hands of every new believer at your church, look no further! *Simply Following Jesus* provides readers an easy-to-understand look at some of the most important aspects of the Christian faith. Thank you, Robert, for this gift to the church. I can't wait to share it with others!"

Kurt Johnston, pastor of campus development,
Saddleback Church

"Jesus's message was simple and stood in stark contrast to the obtuse and unobtainable message the religious leaders of His day had turned it into. Unfortunately, not much has changed. Jesus's message is still incredibly simple, but the theologians and scholars of our day continue to make it complex and unobtainable. Thankfully, people like Robert Watson brush aside the layers of creative complexity to bring us back to the simplicity of the Bible and Jesus's core message."

Larry Osborne, teaching pastor and kingdom ambassador, North
Coast Church, Vista, California

"If you deeply desire to grow closer to God, *Simply Following Jesus* offers clear guidance for where to start—or where to begin again if you've gone astray—to take your next step of faith by simply following Jesus. This book is so powerful because it's rooted in the original; it doesn't stray from God's Word but uncovers the layers of life-changing truth that are already in it."

Megan Fate Marshman, pastor and author of *Relaxed*
and *Meant for Good*

"*Simply Following Jesus* are words that perfectly describe the life that we have watched Robert embrace for the close to twenty years we have known him. Besides being a gifted teacher and leader, his lifestyle has been an outstanding example of following Jesus faithfully, consistently, and simply in a world that is filled with so much complexity."

Pastors Mike & Michelle Tessendorf,
co-founders, Orchard: Africa

"I've had the privilege of serving Jesus with Robert Watson for the last twenty years. What I love about this book is how Robert doesn't just write about these things, he lives them. The infinite, eternal God has revealed Himself in Jesus. You can get to know Him and follow Him! God is not out of reach, because He came down to reach us. I'm excited for you to go on this journey, and I'm grateful to Robert for his leadership along the way."

Chad Moore, lead pastor, Sun Valley Community Church

"We live in a complicated world, but walking with Jesus was never meant to be filled with overthinking and confusion. Robert Watson holds out the hope of simply walking with Jesus the way God invites us to. This book is a treasure that every believer will benefit from."

Debbie Alsdorf, author of *Ten Minutes with God*

"I've had the privilege of knowing and serving alongside Robert Watson for over twenty years, witnessing firsthand his deep knowledge and genuine heart as he guides new believers in their faith journey. His expertise shines through in *Simply Following Jesus,* and having enjoyed his previous book, *Upside Down Crown,* I can confidently say this book will be an essential and inspiring resource for anyone looking to walk more closely with Jesus."

Grant Botma, bestselling author and Inc. 5000 Fastest Growing Company in America winner

"*Simply Following Jesus* is a powerful tool for anyone's spiritual journey. Even as a longtime follower of Jesus, I found it encouraging, enlightening, and motivating. For the new believer, it's the best tool I've seen for starting out right."

Dr. Craig Smith, lead pastor, Mission Hills Church

"Robert Watson has done us a great favor in writing *Simply Following Jesus*. He wrote the book for new believers, but any believer will grow in their faith as they read and reflect on the practices and principles Robert discusses in the book."

Dr. John Vawter, author of *Uncommon Graces*, former president of Phoenix Seminary and Western Seminary

"*Simply Following Jesus* clarifies the complexity out of what many claim religion to be. Living for Jesus goes far beyond the boxes we dutifully check to an abundance we can't possibly imagine. I highly recommend reading this book because it not only encourages somebody who is new to their faith in Jesus but it is also an incredible reminder for those of us who have walked with Him for years!"

Chris Simning, speaker and author of the autobiography *Scribbles*

"*Simply Following Jesus* is a solid resource for churches that are restoring their health and growth. New believers will understand what a relationship with Christ is and how to deepen their relationship with Him. Those who are longtime believers will focus on their relationship with Christ as opposed to being involved in churchianity."

Gary L. McIntosh, distinguished affiliate professor, Talbot School of Theology, Biola University

SIMPLY
FOLLOWING
JESUS

SIMPLY FOLLOWING JESUS

PRACTICES FOR LIVING OUT AN UNCOMPLICATED FAITH

ROBERT WATSON

BakerBooks

a division of Baker Publishing Group
Grand Rapids, Michigan

© 2025 by Robert Watson

Published by Baker Books
a division of Baker Publishing Group
Grand Rapids, Michigan
BakerBooks.com

Printed in the United States of America

Library of Congress Cataloging-in-Publication Data
Names: Watson, Robert (Pastor), author.
Title: Simply following Jesus : practices for living out an uncomplicated faith / Robert Watson.
Description: Grand Rapids, Michigan : Baker Books, a division of Baker Publishing Group, 2025. | Includes bibliographical references.
Identifiers: LCCN 2024036379 | ISBN 9781540904553 (paper) | ISBN 9781540904942 (casebound) | ISBN 9781493450411 (ebook)
Subjects: LCSH: Faith—Religious aspects—Christianity. | Christian life. | Jesus Christ.
Classification: LCC BV4637 .W364 2025 | DDC 248.4—dc23/eng/20250109
LC record available at https://lccn.loc.gov/2024036379

Published in association with Books & Such Literary Management, www.booksandsuch.com.

Baker Publishing Group publications use paper produced from sustainable forestry practices and postconsumer waste whenever possible.

25   26   27   28   29   30   31   7   6   5   4   3   2

To Lindsay
For showing me over the years
what it simply means to love.

CONTENTS

Part 3: Simple Relationships

Introduction

Simple Faith

When I first came to faith in Jesus, I quickly found myself overwhelmed by the myriad of traditions, denominations, styles, and teachings all found under the broad umbrella of "Christianity." For years I questioned if the way I was taught to follow Jesus was the right way. In Bible college and seminary, we debated almost every topic imaginable, opening the door to more questions than answers.

For two thousand years, people have been following Jesus, but in recent history it feels as though we have overcomplicated it. As I look at the teachings and example of Jesus, following Him was never meant to be complicated. Jesus had a way of taking all of life's complexity and brilliantly boiling it down to simple principles that apply universally. In my role as a pastor, I have had the opportunity to walk alongside people who are brand-new to following Jesus. What I have learned is that real faith is not some mystical feeling or intellectual agreement. Real faith is action oriented. And the best way to put faith into action is through simple steps.

Throughout this book, we will look at Jesus's teachings and how to simply apply them in our everyday journey. We will begin by understanding the foundations of our faith. From there, we will unpack the time-tested habits Jesus invites us to follow. Finally, we will look at how Jesus's teachings apply to our relationships and life's purpose. My goal is that no matter your background—whether you are brand-new to faith, still exploring faith, or have been practicing faith for years—these chapters will be simple and applicable.

When challenged with the complicated world of theoretical physics, Albert Einstein once said, "Everything must be made as simple as possible, but not one bit simpler."[1] Throughout *Simply Following Jesus*, we will go on a journey of making everything related to following Him as simple as possible, but not one bit simpler. We will simplify what church history has made complex but without taking away from it. My prayer is that these chapters will strengthen your faith as you follow Jesus one simple step at a time.

SIMPLE
FOUNDATIONS

[1]

Simple Guide

Your word is a lamp to guide my feet
and a light for my path.

Psalm 119:105 NLT

Have you ever traveled to a place you knew little to nothing about? Early in our marriage, my wife and I were generously gifted a vacation to Maui from a longtime family friend. We had one week to enjoy paradise, but where should we explore? It could take months, or even years, to discover all the hidden gems of the island, and we had only six days. We searched travel blogs, social media, excursion reviews, and Google Maps. All of these served as guides to teach us what we didn't know, but the best guide is the one we found on our second day on the island: Maui Ken. Ken had a last name, but I never caught it, so he remains in my phone to this day as "Maui Ken." Ken had spent his life exploring every corner of the island, and he was eager to share his knowledge and, at times, even accompanied us to ensure we made the most of every day. This vacation remains one of our favorites to this day.

What makes a great guide is that they know things you would never know on your own. They understand you, how you are wired, what you will enjoy, and they can show you the way. They have walked the path, learned the lessons—both good and bad—and are now passing along the best experiences. Life is an adventure and an opportunity, but our time here is limited. And to make matters worse, the journey is full of more pitfalls, dead ends, wrong turns, and empty promises than we can imagine. But God is the greatest guide. He knows what we would never know on our own. He understands our nature, our purpose in His creation, and what will truly satisfy the deepest longings of our souls. But more importantly, He has shown us the way to what Jesus refers to as "life to the fullest" (John 10:10 CEB). One of the primary ways God guides us is through the Bible. In this chapter, we will unpack what makes the Bible unique and how to let it serve as our guide on our travel through life.

Not Just Another Book

Before we go any further, I would like to acknowledge that the Bible is complex, more complex than any other book written in the history of humankind. Picture a Bible in your mind. Maybe you have one in your possession; maybe you have seen one on TV or at a relative's house. The Bible that I picture is a large leather-bound book containing over a thousand gilded pages with tiny ribbons spilling out of the bottom to mark passages for quick navigation. Maybe you are picturing a Bible on your phone that opens to a verse of the day, reading plans, or a table of contents. What you are picturing is more than just a book; it's actually a collection of sixty-six books or ancient manuscripts. These manuscripts were written by over forty authors in three languages across three continents over a span of more than fifteen hundred years. It is a mix of history, poetry, prophecy, ancient law, wisdom literature, genealogies, and instruction. These facts alone make this book complex. However, despite this diversity, there exists a profound simplicity when viewing the Bible as a whole. Jesus serves as the central thread woven throughout every page, connecting all its elements.

You will not find another book like the Bible. I believe that its very existence is a testament to its validity. The variety of writers includes kings, shepherds, a doctor, a farmer, a tax collector, fishermen, and a tentmaker. Only with divine help could such a collection of writers—spanning time, language, geographical distance, and culture—produce such a cohesive work. Another divine fingerprint is the prevalence of prophecy, or predictions, woven throughout. Thousands of detailed predictions and foreshadowings have already been fulfilled, many of which were fulfilled in the life of Jesus. The Bible is even so bold as to declare that anyone who claimed to have a prophecy from God must be 100 percent accurate; otherwise they were a false prophet, punishable by death in the Old Testament law (Deut. 18:20–22).

The Bible has maintained perfect accuracy in its prophecies up to this point; some prophecies remain to be fulfilled with the future return of Jesus. Only with the help of God who exists beyond time and can comprehend the entire timeline of history—past, present, and future simultaneously—could authors be inspired to write with clarity and authority beyond their limited understanding. Not to downplay human skills and abilities, but we could not have come up with such a book on our own. Through a miraculous work, God inspired individuals to write exactly what they wrote. As you study the brilliance of the themes, structures, genres, symbolism, and interconnectedness of the Bible, you begin to see that although there were many writers there is one Architect behind it all. This is why the Bible is referred to as "the Word of God."

The Bible speaks of itself in no uncertain terms. Paul, who God inspired to write a portion of the Bible, gives this assurance to a young pastor named Timothy: "All Scripture is God-breathed and is useful for teaching, rebuking, correcting and training in righteousness, so that the servant of God may be thoroughly equipped for every good work" (2 Tim. 3:16–17).

Misusing the Bible

Sadly, there have been many throughout history who have used the Bible to manipulate, control, or oppress people, claiming divine authority over man-made purposes. You may be wondering how something like the Bible, a collection of God-inspired writings, could ever be used for evil. But it has happened throughout human history. The first time it occurred was in perfect paradise after the creation of humankind. In the garden of Eden, the serpent (also referred to as Satan, the tempter, the accuser, and the adversary) twisted God's words to manipulate Eve into doing the one thing she was commanded not to do. The result of Adam and Eve's rebellion is what would forever be referred to as the fall of humankind.

In the Gospel of Luke, Jesus faces a similar temptation. On the verge of beginning His public ministry, Luke records that after forty days of fasting, Jesus faced a series of temptations from Satan. Satan led Him to the top of the temple in Jerusalem and began to quote the Bible to Him, hoping that, even if just for a moment, Jesus would step aside from God's will, forever losing His perfect standing necessary for our salvation. Jesus doesn't fall for it. Instead, He combats Satan's attempt to weaponize the Bible into a tool of manipulation by keeping the verse in the context of the rest of the Bible.

Unfortunately, throughout history we have allowed the complexity of what the Bible *is* to distract us from the simplicity of what it *says*. Whenever we leverage its complexities to serve our man-made agendas, we move backward, not forward. For centuries, institutions placed themselves as the mediator between the common person and the Bible, leveraging unfamiliar Latin or the people's illiteracy to make the Bible say whatever they wanted it to say. While speaking the words of the Bible in a foreign language or archaic dialect may be beautiful, it's not as helpful as when we understand it in our own simple and clear language. When we use obscure or partial passages to weaponize the Bible or try to supplement it with additional revelations, we get dark moments such as the crusades, inquisitions, indulgences, oppression, clinic bombings, hate crimes, witch trials, cults, racism, give-money-to-get-more-money prosperity teachings, and a long litany of theological practices that run completely contrary to the simple teachings of the Bible. A common error today is to use the Bible like a pair of binoculars to look at everyone around us and point out their wrongdoings. The real purpose of the Bible is for us to use it as a mirror to truly see ourselves and to allow it to guide us in reflecting God's love to the world.

God's Preserved Gift

The Bible was given to us as a gift. Despite countless efforts to distort and destroy the Bible throughout history, God has preserved it so that we might personally know Him, His love for us, and the truth that brings eternal freedom (John 8:31–32). In ancient times, God used the office of the scribes who painstakingly transcribed word-for-word manuscripts of the Bible. Some had speculated that the original writings were lost in translation over many centuries until discoveries such as the Dead Sea Scrolls (ancient manuscripts predating the time of Jesus) proved that what we have today is what was written then. The original content was preserved.

The Reformation of the 1500s was primarily driven by a belief that people should have access to the Bible as an authoritative guide for faith. Fueled by the new technology of the printing press, theologians such as Martin Luther, John Calvin, William Tyndale, and Huldrych Zwingli risked their lives to help make the Bible accessible to the people. Today, digital technology has given us unprecedented access to translations, paraphrases, and commentaries. But some still find the Bible complex and overwhelming.

Great for us, the Divine Author who guided the earthly writers came to us and made simple what we made complex. His name is Jesus. Jesus is the King of simplicity (we will discuss this further in the next chapter). The religious leaders of Jesus's time added libraries of additional complex rules far beyond what God had given to us in the Bible. These additional rules were oppressive and served to raise the religious leaders to the top of the hierarchy by pushing everyone else down. Jesus brought clarity to the complexity and unraveled the tightly woven webs of religious misinformation.

Words of Life

I've spent most of my life studying the Bible. I've studied it through church, personal reading, Bible college, and seminary. I study it every week to learn new things about myself, God, faith, humanity, and how life works. And I study it to share it with thousands who, like me, want to learn from it, apply it, and experience the abundant life of joy that comes as a result. Even if my vocation didn't require me to read it constantly, I still would! It's *that* good. In this book are the answers to life's biggest questions, and in it we find the words of eternal life.

If you are reading this and consider the Bible to be just another religious book on the shelf, I assure you—it's not. Together, in the chapters that follow, we will apply the principles found in this book to different areas of life, and we will experience the life we were created for. At the beginning of each chapter, you will find a key verse from the Bible that summarizes the principle being covered. A practice I recommend is memorizing these verses in order to build your foundation of faith rooted in God's Word. By memorizing Scripture, you always carry with you a simple guide to help show you the greatest way.

QUESTIONS FOR REFLECTION AND DISCUSSION

Have you ever had a good guide? What makes a guide good at what they do?

Do you view the Bible as complex or simple?

How does God guide us through the pages of Scripture?

How have you knowingly or unknowingly misused the Bible?

How has the Bible transformed your life for good?

Simple King

For in Christ all the fullness of the Deity lives in bodily form.

Colossians 2:9

When we hear the word "simple," we often think of unintelligent, one dimensional, or boring. That is not the definition we are using in this book. By "simple" we mean straightforward, uncomplicated, unveiled, and clear. Jesus was clear in His identity, message, and mission to the world. In this chapter, we will begin to explore who Jesus is and what He stood for. Faith, at its core, has an object and an action. If you are sitting in a chair right now, you have faith in your chair (object) that it will hold you up (action). Jesus is the object of our faith, and the action is that He gives life. The writer of Hebrews defines faith as "confidence in what we hope for and assurance about what we do not see" (11:1). Our confidence rests in the person and work of Jesus.

God in the Flesh

Did you ever make a diorama in elementary school? One of those little shoeboxes full of little figurines depicting scenes of a story, nature, or town? Now imagine if those little figurines were conscious and intelligent, but all they knew or could see was what existed inside the box. It could be, as they looked at the evidence within the box, that they conclude there was some kind of creative designer behind their little shoebox world. They may even reason that their world couldn't have created itself and that there seems to be a deliberate order to the things they observe. But how could they possibly know you (the creator), your world, or why they were made in the first place?

It would be impossible for the little figurines to figure out the universe on their own from their limited perspective within the box. Somehow, you would have to reveal those things to them. You could deliver a message, or a series of messages, revealing how and why their world was made. You could reveal things about yourself in a way that they could comprehend. Now imagine, in a great act of humility, you made yourself like one of these figurines inside the box. From here, you could really begin to reveal who you are, the world beyond the box, and the purpose for which these figurines were created. For those who would trust you, you could teach them how to live in light of reality beyond the box, a world where everything isn't being held together with Elmer's glue.

God is unlike any other. He is infinite and unbound. He teaches us through the Bible that there is something unique about His nature where He is three and yet one. The theological word for this is trinity or tri-unity. Dr. Wayne Grudem succinctly defines this doctrine: "God eternally exists as three persons, Father, Son, and Holy Spirit, and each person is fully God, and there is one God."[1] If you want to know who this infinite God is, the realities of His kingdom, and the purpose for which you were made, look to Jesus. Jesus is God revealed to us in human form. One of the writers of the Bible puts it this way when he implores Jesus's followers to adopt the same humble mindset as Jesus: "Who, being in very nature God, did not consider equality with God something to be used to his own advantage; rather, he made himself nothing by taking the very nature of a servant, being made in human likeness" (Phil. 2:6–7). Jesus came to provide a way for us to be in a right relationship with God and to show us the way to "life to the fullest" (John 10:10 CEB). But He also came to correct false teaching and to confront false teachers.

Religious Opposition

The religious leaders of Jesus's day (broken into factions known as the scribes, Pharisees, and Sadducees) were frustrated with Jesus because He essentially stripped them of their man-made authority. They had assumed the role of arbiter between God and humankind as "gatekeepers." I use quotation marks because the "gate" was an imaginary one, created for control, and used to distance humanity from God, whether through religious pride or irreligious shame. But Jesus confronted them and cleared a path between God and people for His love and grace to be poured out.

One day, the religious leaders ganged up to try trapping Jesus with their words (and they were masterful with words). First came the Pharisees, top of the socioreligious food chain, and their topic of choice was money and politics. They asked, "Is it right to pay the imperial tax to Caesar or not?" (Matt. 22:17). By asking this question, the Pharisees were trying to divide Jesus's followers and therefore His influence. But the Pharisees never stood a chance against the Author of all things. Matthew continues:

> But Jesus, knowing their evil intent, said, "You hypocrites, why are you trying to trap me? Show me the coin used for paying the tax." They brought him a denarius, and he asked them, "Whose image is this? And whose inscription?"
>
> "Caesar's," they replied.
>
> Then he said to them, "So give back to Caesar what is Caesar's, and to God what is God's." (Matt. 22:18–21)

Matthew records their response to Jesus: "When they heard this, they were amazed. So they left him and went away" (v. 22). In other words, had there been a microphone, Jesus would have held it out in front and dropped it. Battle over.

Next came the Sadducees, a highly influential sect of the religious hierarchy who did not believe in a resurrection. The Sadducees, like the Pharisees, were adorned with priestly garments to leave no doubt of their superiority. While the Pharisees tried to trip Jesus up with a question about political allegiance, the Sadducees sought to trip Him up with a question about marital allegiance. Jesus responds with words that would have caused an audible gasp among the crowds: "You are in error because you do not know the Scriptures [the Bible] or the power of God" (v. 29). For all their so-called expertise, they completely misunderstood the simple truth of the Bible. And if the whole point of the Bible is to guide us to an eternal relationship with God, they completely missed the point there as well. These leaders denied there could ever be life after death. No eternal relationship. No heaven. Once again, Jesus confronts the false teachers and they are left speechless, completely disarmed of their manipulative words. Jesus's ministry would be marked by similar encounters with the religious leaders, each ending in similar fashion. Jesus spoke with authority because He is the Author of all things. There was no use in trying to trap Jesus in their religious nets.

The Greatest Commandment

The Pharisees and Sadducees were totally independent and extremely antagonistic toward one another, but in a rare collaboration, they worked together to discredit Jesus. Like a tag team battle, when the Sadducees stepped out, the Pharisees stepped back in. One of them, an expert in the Old Testament law, poses this question to Jesus: "Teacher, which is the greatest commandment in the Law?" (Matt. 22:36). It was obvious at this point; Jesus wasn't endorsing the complex web of rules these religious leaders had tightly woven like a suffocating blanket over the people. Perhaps they could get Him to lean in just enough to entangle Him in it.

But Jesus, already knowing their hearts, traditions, beliefs, and intentions, always stayed steps ahead of them. Jesus never hesitated in His responses because He simply spoke the truth.

There were no real traps for Him to avoid, webs to spin, or topics to sidestep. And it confounded the religious leaders. Just as darkness is simply the absence of light, lies are simply the absence of truth. And just as darkness has no defense against light, the religious leaders had no defense against the truth revealed by Jesus.

When asked which is the greatest commandment, Jesus replied, "Love the Lord your God with all your heart and with all your soul and with all your mind. This is the first and greatest commandment. And the second is like it: 'Love your neighbor as yourself.' All the Law and the Prophets hang on these two commandments" (vv. 37–40).

Love God. Love people. That is the Bible in a nutshell. Jesus is the King of simplicity.

The Supremacy of Love

How effective would I be as a husband, father, pastor, neighbor, or friend if I knew everything the Bible said but didn't love God or people? When I was in high school, I began to seriously study theology and apologetics (using evidence, reason, and logic to defend the faith). I absorbed book after book of information. At the time, a new internet platform had emerged called "chat rooms." Chat rooms were essentially text-thread conversations around a designated topic that anyone could join in real time.

One such chat room was designated for atheists. Users from all over the world would join in to discuss their reasons for atheism and their disdain for those who believed in God. I would join the group and launch into a debate, me versus everyone, on why God must exist. I could barely keep up with the vehement barrage of responses. After about an hour or so of arguing, I would log out for the day and then repeat the process the following day.

Looking back, I now realize I had lots of great information but no love and no impact. Like the preacher on the street corner with a bullhorn shouting at people walking by, no lives were changed, and if anything, they were just pushed further away from experiencing the true love of God. The Bible teaches that we can have all the knowledge in the world and the eloquence of angels, but if we don't have love we are like "a resounding gong or a clanging cymbal" (1 Cor. 13:1). You will never hear a riveting cymbal solo at the symphony. Just as cymbals do not function unaccompanied by an orchestra, faith does not function unaccompanied by love. Love is essential to faith.

Jesus sums up thousands of years of history and over a thousand pages of writing in a few sentences. All of the Bible hangs on these two commandments: love God and love your neighbor. If you understand this, you understand the Bible. As we will discuss in the next chapter, before we can begin to share this kind of love, we must start by receiving.

QUESTIONS FOR REFLECTION AND DISCUSSION

Jesus says that the Bible's instructions can be simplified down to loving God and loving people. How does this challenge the way you read and understand the Bible?

If you could ask Jesus any one question, what would it be?

Why do you think God revealed Himself to us through a person?

How did Jesus's responses to the religious leaders challenge their belief system? How do His words challenge us today?

Is there an area of your life that is particularly complex? If so, how can the simple truth of Jesus cut through the complexity?

[3]

Simple Salvation

God saved you by his grace when you believed. And you can't take credit for this; it is a gift from God. Salvation is not a reward for the good things we have done, so none of us can boast about it.

Ephesians 2:8–9 NLT

In this chapter, we will explore the foundation of faith that everything else is built upon. It is something called the "gospel," which literally means "good news." The gospel is where our faith begins, and as we grow in our relationship with God, it is where our faith must always come back to. It is the filter through which we interpret every aspect of faith and life. The gospel is the accomplished mission of Jesus, and it is the invitation God gives to each of us and everyone in the world around us to receive. The path to salvation is simple, but the creation of that path was not easy. The Bible teaches that we are saved by grace. Grace is a gift. It is not earned; it's received. If you had to do something to earn it, by definition, it would no longer be a gift. But even though that gift is easy to receive, it came at an unfathomable cost to Jesus.

Free Yet Costly

I have a pastor friend who years ago took a trip with his wife to Poland. They knew that her family had come from Poland, but they knew very little other than the family name. My friend surprised his wife by planning a stop at a city hall in the town where her family was allegedly from to see if they could learn more about her lineage. When they presented what information they had, they were met with shocked silence. The official left without saying much and returned with a small brigade of officials including the mayor. They studied the records and confirmed that she was a direct descendant of the lost royal family, thought to have completely died off three hundred years earlier. Her family had ruled this region for hundreds of years before fleeing as refugees during the Thirty Years' War in the 1600s. The family line eventually found its way to Iowa where their history that they were once a prominent family in Poland became lore. This impromptu stopover in a small-town city hall led to the discovery that they were heirs to castles and a hunting lodge curated by the Polish government, and they were reinstated as Polish nobility. They now use their new-found influence to help share the good news being discussed in this chapter with the people of Poland.

We may be tempted to think, "Well that was an easy way to become foreign nobility!" And in one sense, we would be right. It was easy to receive. But think of all the years it took for a family to rise to such prominence and then to rule, protect, fight, flee, live as refugees, and preserve the family lineage. They received the fruit of what cost countless lives and hundreds of years of perseverance. This gift was easy to receive but came at a great cost. Just because something is easily received does not mean it was easily achieved. So it is with our salvation. Salvation is a great gift that came at a great cost.

Good News

A few years ago, I was working with the team at my church that oversees all our kids' ministries. Our church has more than one location, so it makes for a large team. Throughout the year, we share the good news with the kids of what Jesus accomplished for them, and we invite them to place their faith in Him. We wanted to be consistent as a team, so we set out to simplify how we shared the good news without oversimplifying the depth of the message. Looking at the entire narrative of the Bible from cover to cover with regard to how we are saved, there are five words that can sum it up:

Problem
Plan
Accomplishment
Invitation
Response

The Problem

Before we can understand the good news, we first need to understand the bad news. Here is the bad news: All of us have rebelled against God. We don't need to cover everything on the list (lying, stealing, greed, etc.) to know that we all have broken God's laws. The word for our rebellion is "sin." Just like a good judge wouldn't ignore the actions of a criminal, God won't just ignore sin because He is just. The consequence of sin is death both physically and spiritually. Spiritual death includes separation from God who is holy. Since sin is a part of our very nature, God won't just destroy all sin because that would mean destroying us. Therein lies our problem.

The Plan

The Bible could have ended with the story of our rebellion and all the messy consequences of sin that followed. It would be a pretty quick read. Less like a book and more like a pamphlet. But the story didn't end there because of the core of who God is. God is love and He loves us. He loves you, no matter who you are, what you have done, or what has been done to you. Therefore, God put in motion a plan to resolve the tension between His justice and His love. As soon as sin entered the world, God had a plan to restore what had been broken. Throughout the pages of the Old Testament, God reveals His plan. The plan, and the overarching message of the entire Old Testament, is this: A Savior is coming.

The Accomplishment

God came to us in the person of Jesus and lived the perfect life that none of us were capable of living. Then He gave

His life as a payment for our sin, a sacrifice on our behalf. On the third day after His death, Jesus rose from the dead, a declaration that justice had been satisfied on our behalf and that death had been defeated. Salvation was never something we could accomplish on our own because nobody can live a perfect life. Jesus did what only He could do. He took upon Himself the punishment that we all deserved, satisfying both the love of God and His justice. God doesn't ignore sin; that would be unjust. So Jesus took the payment upon Himself out of incredible love for you and for me.

The Invitation

Through His death and resurrection, Jesus offers life to whomever would receive it through faith in Him. This is the good news. Even though you and I sin, Jesus paid for that sin and offers us new life through faith in Him as our Savior and our Leader. But He doesn't force us to put our trust in Him. We can go on trusting in other things such as our own effort or trusting that none of this is true or really happened, but He invites us all to put our trust in Him as our Savior and our Leader. He describes it as knocking on the door of our life (Rev. 3:20). If we choose to receive Him, He will come into our life and make everything new (21:5).

The Response

Nobody can respond to the invitation but you. I can't respond for you any more than I can respond for my kids, my neighbors, or any other human on the planet. I can only choose to respond for myself. And the same is true for you. Paul, who met Jesus after His resurrection, wrote much of the New Testament in the form of letters to churches that formed after receiving the gospel message. He writes to one of these churches very clearly and simply, "If you declare with your mouth, 'Jesus is Lord,' and believe in your heart that God raised him from the dead, you will be saved" (Rom. 10:9). No work required on our part; that would be religion. What is required of us is faith by which we receive His grace. We choose whether to believe and receive His invitation.

Your Invitation

This is the good news. Even though you and I are sinners, Jesus paid for our sin and offers us new life through faith in Him. We see this in the Gospel of John. Before Jesus raised a man by the name of Lazarus from the dead, Jesus spoke with his sister Martha. "Jesus said to her, 'I am the resurrection and the life. The one who believes in me will live, even though they die; and whoever lives by believing in me will never die. Do you believe this?'" (John 11:25–26). It is an invitation for all of us to put our trust in Jesus.

Do you want to put your faith in Jesus?

You can offer this simple prayer as a response to your decision to say yes to His invitation:

Jesus, I can't solve my problem of sin on my own, so I trust You to rescue me. Thank You for paying all my sin penalty for me and making me right with God forever. Jesus, You are Lord. Lead me from this day forward.

If you would like, you can conclude your prayer with the simple word "Amen," which has been used for thousands of years and means "let it be so."

Living Free

The chapters that follow may feel like a bunch of to-dos, but they are not. They are a bunch of "to believes." To believe that God's way is the best way. To trust in His design over our own desires. These chapters will articulate the principles of God's design, and then it will be up to us to decide whether we will trust God in those areas. This is what we call faith, and faith is action oriented. It requires effort, but it's not about earning.

The goal is not to burden us but to remind us that we have been set free by the grace of God when we put our faith in Jesus. We are free now, and the choice lies in whether we will live in that freedom. This always begins with faith. Faith is the conduit through which the grace of God flows into our lives. It was through faith that the grace of God made us spiritually alive again, and it is through faith that God's grace continues to pour into every area of our lives, not just someday in heaven but also here and now on earth.

You are completely and fully loved by God right now. But the degree to which we will experience the benefits of His love and grace is directly connected to the faith we choose to put into practice each day. Jesus came so that we might have life to the fullest. The full life comes through simple faith, put into practice day by day.

QUESTIONS FOR REFLECTION AND DISCUSSION

Why do you think our tendency is to try to earn our salvation by "being a good person"?

What is faith? How do you see it in your everyday life?

God could have chosen any means for us to receive salvation. Why do you think He chose faith as the conduit?

When was the moment you decided to put your faith in Jesus? If you haven't yet, what is keeping you from putting your faith in Him?

PART 2

SIMPLE HABITS

[4]

Simple Prayer

> And pray in the Spirit on all occasions with all kinds of
> prayers and requests. With this in mind, be alert and
> always keep on praying for all the Lord's people.
>
> Ephesians 6:18

In this chapter, we will learn some helpful tools from Jesus on how to pray and how to keep prayer from becoming stagnant. Prayer has always existed in some form throughout human history. Prayer, by definition, is communication with God. God created prayer to foster relationship with His creation, not so we could bring Him our long checklist of requests. Author Anne Lamott brilliantly simplifies some of the most common, yet powerful, prayers into just three words: "help, thanks, wow."[1] Behind each word is a wide range of human emotions and raw expression, yet these prayers are simple enough that even a small child learning to speak can pray them. As God designed it, the natural outcome of prayer is relational growth. Communication is vital for relationships, and prayer is one of God's greatest gifts for deepening our relationship with Him. Jesus recognized our tendency to complicate or overwhelm ourselves when finite beings communicate with an infinite God.

How to Pray

The Gospels record many instances of Jesus praying. On one such occasion, Jesus gathered a large crowd on a hillside in Galilee and taught them how to pray. He presented an example of prayer that is widely known and easily memorized. Even if you haven't grown up around church, there's a good chance you've heard this prayer portrayed in a movie or at a football game, funeral, wedding, or meal. This is how Jesus teaches us to pray:

> Our Father in heaven,
> hallowed be your name,
> your kingdom come,
> your will be done,
>   on earth as it is in heaven.
> Give us today our daily bread.
> And forgive us our debts,
>   as we also have forgiven our debtors.
> And lead us not into temptation,
>   but deliver us from the evil one. (Matt. 6:9–13)

If we're not careful, we might turn Jesus's prayer example into a ritual. For those of us accustomed to reciting it, it can become automatic. However, Jesus offers this prayer as a guide, not the ultimate destination. In other instances in the Bible, Jesus doesn't recite this prayer; instead, His prayers are *relational* rather than *ritualistic*. Let's identify some key principles of simple prayer from Jesus:

> Praise God for who He is ("hallowed [meaning holy or revered] be your name").
> Submit our ways to His ("your will be done").
> Ask for help ("give . . . forgive . . . lead . . . deliver").

TACOS

When my kids were first learning to pray, our prayer times on the way to school, before meals, or before bed started turning into the exact same recited prayer, which is completely normal. But we wanted to break free from the ritual and routine of it. There are lots of different kinds of prayers we can pray that God models and teaches throughout the Bible. In the Old Testament, God was worshiped in the temple, and the people of Israel were instructed to "enter his gates with thanksgiving and his courts with praise; give thanks to him and praise his name" (Ps. 100:4). In the New Testament, John—one of Jesus's closest friends and a disciple—writes, "If we confess our sins, he is faithful and just to forgive us our sins and to cleanse us from all unrighteousness" (1 John 1:9 ESV). As it is with all relationships, conversations can take on many forms and topics as we have just seen. One way to help us remember the different topics of prayer is with the use of acrostics. The one that is the easiest to remember with my kids is TACOS.

Thanksgiving is expressing gratitude for what God has done.

Adoration is praising God for who He is.

Confession is being honest with God about our challenges.

Others is about the needs of those in our lives or on our hearts.

Self is about those things that are on our mind for ourselves.

My kids quickly picked up the TACOS prayer method. To help us break up the monotony and ritual of prayer times, we put the Scrabble letters T, A, C, O, S, and the blanks in a little baggy. When it came time to pray, we drew squares. Whatever letter we selected, that determined the kind of prayer we prayed. If we drew a blank square, we got to choose!

It's so easy to only focus on ourselves when we pray. TACOS helps us to break free from self-focused prayer. Yes, God cares about our challenges, needs, and desires. But prayer, like relationships, requires dialogue between two people. Treating God like He is a cold, distant genie makes prayer a one-way street. Beginning prayer with thanksgiving immediately redirects our focus away from ourselves, allowing us to perceive the bigger picture. Even in difficult times, there's always something to be grateful for, even if it's simply the assurance that the challenges we face are temporary. Recent studies have discovered that the human brain cannot simultaneously operate with gratitude and anxiety; it can only focus on one at a time.[2] This is why Paul writes to the Philippians, "Do not be anxious about anything, but in every situation, by prayer and petition, with thanksgiving, present your requests to God.

And the peace of God, which transcends all understanding, will guard your hearts and your minds in Christ Jesus" (Phil. 4:6–7). Paul offers prayers mixed with gratitude as an alternative to anxiety.

Fighting Anxiety

Almost 20 percent of Americans struggle with anxiety disorders, the most common form of mental illness.[3] I also used to struggle with debilitating anxiety attacks. When I shared this with my grandmother, who had been following Jesus for over half a century, she gave me a homework assignment. She said, "The next time you feel an anxiety attack coming on, I want you to pray." I told her, "Of course I will pray; that's typically my first response. When you feel like you are dying, God is on speed dial." But then she clarified, "Not for yourself." *What?!* In those moments, all I can think about is myself. She continued, "I want you to pray for somebody else. You can choose whoever you want, but I want you to petition God on their behalf." She gave me some suggestions of who I could be praying for and then sent me on my way.

When my next anxiety attack began, I started praying for my uncle and his ministry. I prayed for my neighbor who didn't yet know Jesus. Random people came to mind, and I prayed for them too. What began as a defense quickly shifted to offense. Even if I died in the process, I was going to fight back. Without even realizing it, the attack was gone, but I continued to fight with prayer.

When I reported back to my grandma, she told me that sometimes attacks or ailments are merely physiological. Sometimes they are psychological. And sometimes they are spiritual. And it's not always easy to tell which one we are facing. Regardless of the cause, if we use the symptoms as a trigger to pray, what was once destructive becomes constructive. If it's a spiritual attack, the enemy hates when we pray; and if we pray every time he attacks—well, he will stop attacking. If it's psychological, then praying for others will break us free from the downward spiral. If it's physiological, it's always good to talk with the Great Physician (God) while we are on our way to the doctor. My grandmother helped me turn a losing situation into a win-win.

As I reflected on this experience, it became apparent that my natural tendency when I was stressed or anxious was to turn inward. Imagine the posture of lowering your head in such a moment. What can you see? All I could see was myself in those moments. To express gratitude or praise God or pray for others, I must lift my head. This may sound too elementary, but there is power in perspective. Now I can see beyond my immediate circumstances. Now I can see that I am not alone in my struggle, I can see that God has been faithful, and I can see that the story is not done being written.

Praying with Others

While it is important to pray *for* others, it is also important to pray *with* others. One of the beautiful benefits of prayer is that it not only connects us with God but also with others. My closest relationships are with those for whom I have prayed with a hand on their shoulder and those who have prayed for me with a hand on mine. You are a soul within a body. You are more than just a complex network of cells and synapses; you are a spirit dwelling within a temporary body. Prayer connects us with other spirits, or more accurately, spirit to Spirit to spirit. God is Spirit, and when we pray to Him with and for others, there is an intertwining of spirits.

Perhaps you are new to prayer; if so, the thought of praying out loud with other people might feel overwhelming. I understand the hesitation. Start simple. Begin by praying silently and alone for others. After you feel comfortable doing this, you can start praying aloud for a meal or for a friend or loved one. As you grow in familiarity, begin to venture out. Don't be afraid to look foolish in front of others. Begin to ask God, "Who can I pray for, and how can I pray for them?" As time goes on, the practice of prayer will become natural. I am still learning. Just as communicating with friends and family is a lifelong process, so is communicating with God.

Listening

Another simple prayer that has existed for centuries is a prayer of listening rather than talking. Remember, prayer is relational, and great relationships are a two-way street. The prayer goes like this: "Come, Holy Spirit." And then wait. Wait for God to give you a thought, an encouragement, a truth, something to pray for, and so on. If you start to get distracted, repeat the prayer "Come, Holy Spirit" and continue to wait. My greatest moments of prayer have come not when I was talking but when I was listening.

As with all relationships, the key to prayer is consistency. Relationships are built over time. The more time you spend in conversation with your Father, the more you will get to know Him, and He in turn will help you get to know your true self. It can also be expected that the most powerful moments of prayer are not the moments when we are doing all the talking. Learn to listen. Ask God questions and wait. My wife is my closest friend in the world. If every conversation were just me talking, that wouldn't be much of a relationship, would it? In fact, it wouldn't be a conversation at all.

So pause, listen, and just enjoy being with God even if you're not talking. This is how prayer can be continuous. The apostle Paul describes this type of continuous prayer in his first letter to the Thessalonians: "Rejoice always, *pray continually*, give thanks in all circumstances; for this is God's will for you in Christ Jesus" (5:16–18). Sometimes the prayer is simply, "Thank you, God, for being here with me." As you keep the conversation going, you will learn to discern His voice and you will begin to sense His presence.

There are lots of ways to pray and things to pray about. Start simple. You can even start right now. God is listening, and He would love to talk with you.

QUESTIONS FOR REFLECTION AND DISCUSSION

Prayer can be intimidating. How does the TACOS method help you overcome these challenges?

Why does God guide us to start our worship with thanksgiving?

Which of the five types of prayers do you need to practice more?

How did Jesus demonstrate that prayer is a two-way conversation? How does this challenge how you pray?

Who is somebody you can pray for over the next week?

[5]

Simple Transformation: Lies

Do not conform to the pattern of this world, but be transformed by the renewing of your mind. Then you will be able to test and approve what God's will is—his good, pleasing and perfect will.

Romans 12:2

A process of transformation takes place as we step into a life of faith. This transformation happens in the dominion of the mind in a battle between truth and lies. In this chapter, we will unpack the three sources of lies: from within ourselves, from the world around us, and from an unseen spiritual war. In the following chapter, we'll look at three sources of truth by which we'll be set free: the Word of God (that is, the Bible), the Spirit of God, and the wisdom of God.

Metamorphosis

As a kid, I remember learning about metamorphosis in nature. I recall how biologists made a complicated process sound so simple. They categorized the metamorphosis from caterpillar to butterfly in four stages: egg, larva, pupa, and adult. Simple, isn't it? Perhaps from the outside looking in. But it is in no way easy, especially when considered from the inside. Inside the cocoon, the real transformation is taking place. First, everything is deconstructed, and then it's reconstructed as an entirely new creation, almost unrecognizable from the original.

The cells of the caterpillar are broken down to a sort of cell soup with each cell containing the blueprints of a beautiful, multicolored flying creature vastly different from the squishy caterpillars they once were. Once the cells have been repurposed, the next challenge begins. What once was a protector (the cocoon) is now a cage. As the newly formed wings fill with fluid, they start pushing against the chrysalis, encountering significant resistance. This struggle is part of the design. If we were to intervene and assist the butterfly in escaping its enclosure, we would unintentionally kill it. It's through this resistance that the wings develop the strength necessary for flight. After the reconstruction and overcoming resistance, a new creation emerges, bearing little resemblance to its former self.

A New Creation

To convey the transformation we undergo when we put our faith in Jesus, the Bible uses the Greek word *metamorphoó* (from which we get the word "metamorphosis"). Some of the change we experience is instantaneous in the spiritual realm. When we acknowledge Jesus as Lord and put our trust in His life, death, and resurrection, our once dead spirit is made alive. Our standing before God is transformed from guilty to righteous on par with the righteousness of Jesus. It's as if He wrapped our sin-sick bodies with a robe of His perfection. The Holy Spirit then enters and dwells within us. Paul writes to the church at Corinth, "Therefore, if anyone is in Christ, the new creation has come: The old has gone, the new is here!" (2 Cor. 5:17). But there is another process that begins to radically change us from the inside out. And it too is quite simple yet challenging. We, like the caterpillar, enter a process of transformation that is met with great but necessary resistance.

Battle for the Mind

Our spiritual transformation begins in the mind. This is the same place where our spiritual fall and subsequent death in the garden of Eden began. Before rebellion ever took action, it already existed in the mind. When Satan sought to distort and destroy God's most prized creation, he aimed for the mind. "Did God really say . . . ?" he asked Eve. With that, the tempter called into question the intentions of God. If he could change the thinking of Adam and Eve from "We have everything we need and desire from God" to "Perhaps God is withholding something good from us," then the battle was already won. The original lie is still the most prevalent lie today.

Beginning in the book of Genesis, God is engaged in the task of restoring what sin has destroyed. Although He has taken most of the work upon Himself, He also invites us to work alongside Him. This task involves the renewing of the mind. To play our part in this process, we need to first identify and acknowledge the sources of the lies.

Three Sources of Lies

Lies will always come from one of three sources: from within ourselves, from the world around us, and from an unseen spiritual war.

Within Ourselves

In your lifetime, nobody will lie to you more than *you* will. Every temptation we ever face is attached to a lie we are telling ourselves. Take, for example, the temptation to lust after someone. To justify our sin, we may tell ourselves things such as "If it's only in my mind, it's not going to hurt anyone," "Only they will satisfy what my soul is longing for," "Everybody struggles," or "I'm just following my heart." When actor and comedian Woody Allen left a long-term relationship with Mia Farrow for her daughter (who was thirty-four years his junior), he simply responded with the justification, "The heart wants what it wants."[1] As a fellow pastor often says, "Rationalizing is telling yourself rational lies." He's right, and that's not the worst of it. We are all *experts* at it.

Or maybe you're tempted to gossip. Gossip occurs when you talk *about* another person instead of *to* that person. If I choose to focus on the problems of those around me, it serves as an effective distraction from the more difficult work of dealing with my own issues. Gossip is easy to justify and, in many ways, socially acceptable. Some subtle lies we may tell ourselves to justify gossip are "We are just talking," "We'll keep it between us," "At least I'm not as bad as that person," or "I feel better about myself when I point out the flaws in others." Or perhaps you have heard someone justify the lie by saying, "I'm just sharing this information so we can pray for them."

One last example is the sin of coveting, which is longing for what other people have. Like the other temptations, coveting is a common and prevalent temptation. In fact, God includes it as one of the Ten Commandments in Exodus. Some subtle lies we may tell ourselves to justify coveting are "If only I had that car, I would prove my value," "If I had that house, my life would be perfect," "If I had their relationship, I would be full of joy," or "I deserve that more than they do." Notice where the focus lies in almost all of these examples: *ourselves*. The lie behind the lies is that we are the center of the universe. In his bestselling book *The Purpose Driven Life*, pastor Rick Warren opens with a profound statement: "It's not about you."[2] It's far too easy to lose sight of this reality. When we look back on our story, we think we are the star because we are in every scene. But we are only a part of a much greater story—a story that begins and ends with God. Yet in His grace, He has invited us to join our stories with His.

The World

When I was younger, I used to talk with other guys about sports and activities. I have now entered the phase of life where we talk about what meats we are smoking. I haven't made it to the phase where we talk about various medical issues, but I hear it's coming. Whenever I'm grilling or smoking a pork shoulder, I don't realize I too am absorbing the smell—until I go inside. Entering a smoke-free environment quickly reveals that I am carrying the previous environment with me. It's in my hair, on my clothes, and filling every pore of my skin. So it is with the culture of the world. We are saturated with it, and we don't even know it. Before we move further, we should define what we mean by "culture." Culture is the collective values, language, beliefs, and desires of a group of people. Everyone contributes to this community ethos but none more so than a select few known as "influencers." Through social media and technology, new values and beliefs take flight faster than at any point in history. However, there is one major flaw in this system. Culture is created by people, and people are natural-born rebels. Take my own children as an example. I never had to teach them how to lie, cheat, steal, hurt, or covet; these things came naturally to them.

Not only are we individually rebellious, but we also share a culture of rebellion. And the lies that we collectively share as a culture can often be subtle. Take for example the previous justification for a man marrying someone who was essentially his stepdaughter. "The heart wants what it wants" is a culturally shared mantra. We hear it in music, see it in media feeds, and odds are, we ourselves have said it or some form of it. Sometimes it sounds like "follow your heart" or "live your best life" or "you do you." But they all orbit the same subtle lie: It's all about you. Cultural statements and behaviors are so regularly repeated they become what the Bible refers to as a pattern. This is why Paul writes, "Do not conform to the pattern of this world." While there are some threads of truth woven through many cultural values and beliefs, the natural drift of a culture built by a collective of naturally rebellious people will always move away from God and ultimate truth, not toward Him.

Spiritual War

Every day we are bombarded with stories about wars and rumors of wars. These are apparent to us because we can see them unfolding on the daily news cycle. But there is also an invisible war going on in the spiritual realm. We know this because the Bible gives us glimpses of this activity. Jesus not only acknowledged this reality but also regularly fought against it. Jesus healed those who were demon-possessed. Demons were terrified of Jesus and His ultimate authority. On one occasion, Jesus cast multiple demons out of a man and into a herd of pigs who then ran off a cliff, drowning in the waters below (Matt. 8:28–34). In Western culture, the notion of spiritual forces like the devil or demons often raises eyebrows, with some dismissing them entirely and others attributing everyday inconveniences like flat tires or broken nails to the devil himself. As mentioned earlier, spiritual warfare persists in the same arena introduced in the book of Genesis—an ongoing battle for the mind. Jesus describes the devil's primary tool as lies, identifying him as the originator of deceit (John 8:44).

Through Jesus's interactions with the spiritual realm, we witness individuals affected by demons in various ways, including psychosis, self-harm, speech impairment, unforgiveness, physical and spiritual blindness, deafness, depression, homicidal thoughts, false teachings, seizures, extraordinary strength, and acts of evil. This is not to say that anytime we see one of these symptoms it is demonic activity, as Jesus clarifies during a theological discussion among His disciples about a man born blind (John 9). The accounts of Jesus's ministry differentiate between physical sicknesses and demon possession, even though in some cases the symptoms are the same. Ultimately, all demonic activities oppose God's work. God loves humanity and seeks genuine relationships with us, while Satan and demons strive to destroy or distract us from our need for this relationship and hinder God's work in the world.

The Bible cautions against opening our minds to demonic influences through practices such as fortune-telling, séances, idol worship, or attempting to communicate with the dead, as these practices invite destruction into our lives.

In a world saturated with lies, it is no wonder we buy into them without even realizing it. They are common throughout history, they are common in our culture, and they often even ring true in our hearts. In the next chapter, we will identify the three places we can go to draw from the deep wells of truth available to all of us.

QUESTIONS FOR REFLECTION AND DISCUSSION

Of all the possible battlegrounds, why do you think Satan attacks the mind?

What are some lies about God, the world, or yourself you have believed?

What is something you rationalized in the past, even though you knew it wasn't good?

What transformation have you already begun to see in your life of faith?

[6]

Simple Transformation: Truth

> If you hold to my teaching, you are really my disciples. Then you will know the truth, and the truth will set you free.
>
> John 8:31–32

In the previous chapter, we established the sources of lies as being within ourselves, the world, and an unseen spiritual war. In this chapter, we'll turn our attention to the sources of truth. We live in a culture that believes in "subjective" truth, or truth that changes based on a person's point of view, feelings, or even opinions. You've most likely heard subjective truth expressed through phrases like this: "What's true for you isn't true for me." It's as if we're all going through life in our own separate bubbles, and each bubble has its own definition of reality. Here again we find a familiar lie: "I'm the star of my own story; the master of my own universe." To redirect us away from subjective truth, we need ultimate truth. Only when we draw from the wells of God's Word, God's Spirit, and God's wisdom as our sources of truth will we grow in the timeless truth of the gospel. Whereas lies keep us trapped, the truth sets us free (John 8:32).

God's Word

The Bible is our primary guide for truth. However, because it was written to a range of audiences over a wide span of time and in a variety of literary forms, it does not read like a novel. Many have made the mistake of assuming it should be read from front to back like a regular book. When I first set out to read the entire Bible, I started on the first page with the account of creation. It was a great start, beginning with some of life's biggest questions. But as I went along, I encountered stories of drama, conflict, betrayal, and detailed family histories.

The next book (Exodus) began with one of the greatest stories of rescue and redemption the world has ever seen, but then it shifted suddenly to painstakingly detailed laws and architectural plans. By the third book (Leviticus), my eyes began to glaze over, reading line after line of ancient Jewish civil and ceremonial laws with an occasional pop of history. Many have set out on the same journey as me, and many have tapped out somewhere between the books of Leviticus and Numbers.

While all the Bible is inspired by the Holy Spirit, some parts are more practical in following Jesus than others. I recommend starting with the New Testament book of John. John, an early follower of Jesus, records firsthand the life and ministry of Jesus. The first four books of the New Testament, Matthew, Mark, Luke, and John (known as "the Gospels"), are detailed accounts of Jesus's life and ministry written from four different perspectives and for four different audiences. Matthew was written to Jewish Christians. Mark was written for the Romans. Luke was written primarily to the Greeks. Lastly, the Gospel of John was written to a much broader audience made up of both religious and rebellious individuals. Here is my recommended reading plan for those new to the Bible:

John—An account of the life and ministry of Jesus.

Acts—The account of the arrival of the Holy Spirit and the start of the church.

Galatians, Ephesians, Philippians, Colossians—Four letters written to new believers on how to apply faith to their lives.

James—A how-to book on relationships.

Romans—A deeper dive into understanding the detailed workings of the gospel.

Proverbs—Wisdom literature with thirty-one chapters, perfect for a chapter a day in a month.

Psalms—Poetry and songs to God navigating a wide variety of emotions and situations; I use the book of Psalms as a guide for praying.

This is just a starting point. As you gain a greater understanding of the message and context in which the Bible is written, other books of the Bible will also prove fruitful. As you study, the Holy Spirit will guide you in understanding.

Words on a page will begin to connect with your heart, and the metamorphosis from within will begin to take shape.

God's Spirit

"Immanuel" is more than just a word we sing around Christmas time; it's the primary theme of the Bible. It means "God is with us." When Jesus was with His disciples, He frequently forewarned them of the impending crucifixion but He reassured them not to fret, as the resurrection would follow. He also explained that postresurrection, He would depart once more (the ascension). Then, He made a startling claim. He told them that His departure was actually advantageous for them. *What?!* How could Jesus's absence possibly be beneficial? He clarified that following His ascension: He would send the Holy Spirit, who is God with us.

Unrestricted by time and space, the Holy Spirit, or "Helper" (see John 14:26), accompanies followers of Jesus, providing guidance, teaching, comfort, challenge, empowerment, connection, mediation, and collaboration in the process of transforming the mind. The same Spirit that resurrected Jesus resides within us. The Spirit that hovered over the abyss at creation, infusing life into all living beings, guiding the ancients, inspiring the Scriptures, resurrecting Jesus, empowering the disciples, and effecting transformation throughout history also dwells within you if you have placed your faith in Jesus. He represents God's presence in the contemporary world. Even now, your curiosity about divine matters, yearning for more than worldly offerings, faith in Jesus, burgeoning love for humanity, discontentment with sin, inclination toward prayer, and character transformation can be attributed to the Holy Spirit's work in your life.

Our relationship with the Holy Spirit operates in ways very similar to our earthly relationships. Take for instance my relationship with my wife. Our relationship grows through spending time together, sharing experiences, navigating conflicts, and regular conversations ranging from deeply vulnerable topics to the mundane. I grow in my relationship with the Holy Spirit in some of the same ways. Intentional time with the Holy Spirit can come in many forms: taking a hike, opening the Bible while enjoying a cup of coffee, serving others, listening to music, floating in a pool, or finding a quiet place and closing the door. Each of us are wired differently and will connect with the Holy Spirit in unique ways. However, we are not limited to only the ideal settings. This meaningful time can also be found during a car ride, on a lunch break, while doing yard work, fixing a truck, or even buying groceries. The key lies in being intentional. Brother Lawrence, a seventeenth-century monk, famously found delight in the presence of the Holy Spirit and conversations with God while washing dishes and making sandals. He writes, "The most holy and necessary practice in our spiritual life is the presence of God. That means finding constant pleasure in his divine company, speaking humbly and lovingly with him in all seasons, at every moment, without limiting the conversation in any way."[1]

There is a profound moment in the Old Testament when God chooses to manifest His presence with a prophet named Elijah. God instructs Elijah to stand on the mountain as He (the Lord) passes by. "Then a great and powerful wind tore the mountains apart and shattered the rocks before the LORD, but the LORD was not in the wind. After the wind there was an earthquake, but the LORD was not in the earthquake. After the earthquake came a fire, but the LORD was not in the fire. And after the fire came a gentle whisper. When Elijah heard it, he pulled his cloak over his face and went out and stood at the mouth of the cave" (1 Kings 19:11–13).

We would expect the presence of God to be in the roar of the wind, the shaking of the earth, or in an all-consuming fire, but we instead find Him in a gentle whisper. The Holy Spirit speaks in a whisper, and we live in a world full of noise and distractions. The Holy Spirit invites us into a space where we can push away the distractions and spend time with Him, both talking and listening. And the beautiful thing is that wherever we go, He is with us. This is why we pray, "Come, Holy Spirit." And then do something uncommon in the modern age: wait. If you find yourself distracted, pray it again and wait. Many times, after some time, He will bring something to your mind such as an encouragement, a thought, a person to pray for, a picture, a challenge, or sometimes just the joy and peace of His presence. But He brings it in a whisper.

God's Wisdom

God communicates clearly through His Word and His Spirit. However, what about those moments when we require direction, insight, or understanding, but there is no specific verse addressing the matter and we have not received clear instruction from the Holy Spirit? When you take the principles of Scripture, the understanding of God's heart, and the multitude of experiences of people throughout the ages, both good and bad, you end up with something the Bible calls "more precious than rubies" and "more profitable than silver and . . . gold":

wisdom (Prov. 3:13–15). Wisdom, like the Holy Spirit, will never contradict Scripture. It is important to note that there are two types of wisdom. There is godly wisdom and there is "worldly wisdom." Worldly wisdom may sound wise, but it is foolish. An example would be the maxim "Follow your heart." The Bible warns us that the heart can be deceitful and that our desires can lead us into ruin (Jer. 17:9; 1 Tim. 6:9). This is why having the Bible as a guardrail is so important. Sometimes worldly wisdom is masked with a spiritual sound-ing veneer such as "God helps those who help themselves." Sounds spiritual, right? Well, the Bible teaches that God helps the helpless, which is all of us, and when we were spiritually dead in our sin, God made us alive in Christ by grace through faith with absolutely no works done on our part (Eph. 2:4–5, 8–9). Godly wisdom never contradicts the principles of the Bible because all true wisdom is ultimately God's wisdom. James writes that "wisdom that comes from heaven is first of all pure; then peace-loving, considerate, submissive, full of mercy and good fruit, impartial and sincere" (James 3:17).

Throughout my life I've sought out those who are wise to speak wisdom into my life and decisions. I've lost count of how many times God has revealed His truth to me through the con-duit of godly people. How do you identify a person who can speak truth into your life? Look at the fruit of their life. If you are married, ask yourself, Who has a great marriage, the kind of marriage I hope to have one day? Then seek them out and ask them about what they have learned over the years, what practices have been helpful, or what pitfalls they discovered. If you are a parent of young children and know somebody who has a great relationship with their adult children, seek godly wisdom from them. If you are in a position of leadership, who is a strong leader and exemplifies the characteristics of Jesus? Where there is the fruit of the Spirit, you will find wisdom.

I have learned that wisdom is all around us, but we must seek it. People are busy, and odds are, that couple you desire to learn from isn't going to knock on your door one day and ask to share their precious insights with you. But if you have the courage to ask, godly people are almost always happy to share godly wisdom with others. When you approach somebody in humility and say, "I really admire what I see in your life, and I am growing in how to follow Jesus in my _____ [marriage, work, finances, friendships, etc.]. Would it be okay if I asked you a few questions about what you have learned over the years?," they often will be honored to share with you. Even by asking the question, you are honoring them. The more we marinate our minds on God's Word, listen for His whispers, and seek out godly wisdom from others, the more we will grow in godly wisdom ourselves. Discerning truth will begin to come more naturally, and we can sometimes navigate crossroads with the simple question, What is the wise decision? The more we can think before we act, the more we will walk in true wisdom, and the more the fruit of wisdom will become evident in our own lives.

In the battle against internal lies, worldly deception, and spiritual warfare, God has armed us with His Word, the whispers of the Holy Spirit, and godly wisdom. With this threefold strategy, we capture every thought and align it with Jesus, counter the pervasive falsehoods of society, and collaborate with God to restore what evil has ruined. As we renew our minds, our metamorphosis progresses, leaving behind the old life of the caterpillar for the new life of the butterfly.

QUESTIONS FOR REFLECTION AND DISCUSSION

How does God invite us to play a role in our transformation process?

Of the recommended books of the Bible for starters, is there a particular one that interests you? Why?

Why do you think God's presence was revealed in the "gentle whisper" rather than the windstorm, earthquake, and fire?

What is the difference between godly and worldly wisdom?

Who in your life has demonstrated godly wisdom?

[7]

Simple Greatness

Whoever wants to become great among you must be your servant, and whoever wants to be first must be your slave—just as the Son of Man did not come to be served, but to serve, and to give his life as a ransom for many.

Matthew 20:26–28

As a teenager, I was trying to understand my growing faith, the concept of praying to an all-powerful God, and a nagging sense of longing for something more than I was currently experiencing. At that time, I thought prayer was just a means to get God to do whatever I wanted. I was sixteen years old when I had a very honest, very selfish prayer while driving west on Guadalupe Road in my 1967 Ford Mustang. For some reason, I can recall every detail of this moment, even decades later. I believe it is because God wanted me to remember this prayer, a prayer that He would certainly answer in the most unexpected way. I was in the right-hand lane, talking to God, as I drove past my high school on my way to youth group at church. "God, I want to be great. Like, *really* great. I want to do something awesome that will be remembered and leave the world a different place."

This prayer was completely genuine. In my mind, I imagined the answer to this prayer would be something like writing a hit song. Or I thought I might invent something, cure cancer, make a major scientific discovery, or become the world's best in any field. I was open to suggestions. I laugh when I think back on how self-focused my teenage prayers were, but to a degree, that is all of us even as we get older. I believe God heard me and met me in that place because of how honest I was being. God is not afraid to meet us where we are, even if it's on the corner of Guadalupe and mild narcissism. In this chapter, we will learn from Jesus how to turn our idea of greatness upside down, or rather, right side up.

Seeking Greatness

As it turns out, I'm not the first person to ask God for greatness. Two of Jesus's disciples, James and John, also known as the "Sons of Thunder" (Mark 3:17 ESV), once made a similar request (Matt. 20:20–23; Mark 10:35–40). One of the most shocking things about their request was not the request itself; it was the timing. Jesus had pulled the twelve disciples aside and told them that upon their arrival in Jerusalem, He was going to be arrested, tried, condemned, mocked, beaten, crucified, and on the third day raised back to life! In other words, Jesus had shared some earth-shattering information with them, but instead of expressing shock and awe, the Sons of Thunder ask for greatness. To make matters worse, Matthew records that their mom asks on their behalf. So brave. Jesus just mapped out the most important week in human history, and what is on the mind of these disciples? Themselves. But before we think we would be any better than the disciples, it's important to remember that we have the same human nature. We naturally think about ourselves first and often, and the disciples' human nature is clearly on display. They want to be in the places of honor at Jesus's right and left in the new kingdom. Perhaps they didn't understand what Jesus was saying about the road ahead, or perhaps they were too busy rehearsing their speech in their heads to pay attention. They didn't understand what they were asking for; they just knew they wanted power and prestige.

Have you ever wanted your life to be something great? I think we all do. Look no further than how enamored we are with celebrities, leaders, athletes at the top of their game, and other influencers. According to society, these are the "greats," and we often imagine what it might be like to join their ranks. What if I were to tell you that the secret to greatness is available to you right now? But it might not be what you think. To follow Jesus, we need to invert our thinking. In the Gospels, Jesus regularly took the commonly held thoughts and values of society and culture and flipped them upside down, or from His perspective, right side up. After lovingly denying the request of the Sons of Thunder (by way of Mama Thunder), Jesus gathered His disciples together and explained to them a new definition of greatness. To be great is not to ascend the social or organizational ladder while looking down on those below you. That might be the world's definition, but it isn't God's definition. If that were God's definition of greatness, Jesus never would have willingly gone to Jerusalem. In fact, the events recorded in the Bible never would have happened. No, the world's definition of greatness is totally contrary to the actions of God. God humbled Himself by taking on flesh. He meets us where we are to love and serve us. That is the definition of greatness. It is to elevate others, not ourselves. Jesus explains the world's view of greatness and then with precision and clarity charges them (and us), "Not so with you." He goes on, "Instead, whoever wants to become great among you must be your servant, and whoever wants to be first must be your slave—just as the Son of Man did not come to be served, but to serve, and to give his life as a ransom for many" (Matt. 20:26–28). This is greatness redefined.

A Life Well Lived

I recently officiated the funeral service for my grandmother, Jaye Watson. She was ninety-two when she went to be with Jesus. At the beginning of the service, I read her eulogy, and on paper her life didn't seem very impressive. She married young, stayed home to raise her boys, worked a little here and there, and lived in a modest home with Grandpa. They shared this home for most of her life before dementia and illness eventually caused her to move into assisted care where she passed away. As we prepared for her funeral, we didn't expect many people to show given her age. We ambitiously set up the room for a decent turnout given the size of our family but quickly realized we were thinking too small. We delayed starting as people kept pouring in. We had to scrounge up as many chairs as we could find and build new rows. Even this wasn't enough and so the remaining people stood. The best part of the whole service was the time spent reflecting on her life. Person after person shared stories about the unique ways she served other people. She volunteered her time in hospitals, in schools, and in church. She mentored individuals and couples. She started a Christian bookstore with my grandfather and started counseling local teenagers and adults. One woman even stood up and explained that while she never knew my grandmother, she was named after her because Jaye had led her father to the Lord back in the sixties. She invested her most limited resource, time, into the lives of others. As I listened to these stories, one word kept coming to mind: greatness. This is what Jesus was speaking about to His disciples.

Lift your eyes and look around you. Who can you serve with your time and attention? I finished the service by sharing several verses from my grandmother's Bible, which was almost completely underlined with different colored pencils, each one representing an overarching theme. On the blank pages at the front of her Bible, she had taped and stapled in creeds, names and birthdates of people she was praying for, topical indexes, theological word definitions, and a paper labeled "Quotes I like." As I scanned the quotations, one jumped out at me from an old game show host named Peter Marshall. The quote read, "In truth, the measure of life is not in its duration, but in its donation."

Good Works

My grandmother is one example of someone who finished this journey well. But how do we even start this journey? I believe we begin by seeking God's guidance. In one of the most famous verses of the Bible, Paul writes to the church in Ephesus, "For it is by grace you have been saved, through faith—and this is not from yourselves, it is the gift of God—not by works, so that no one can boast" (Eph. 2:8–9). He continues, "For we are God's handiwork, created in Christ Jesus to do good works, which God prepared in advance for us to do" (v. 10). In other words, we have been rescued by God's amazing grace through faith, not by any effort or work of our own. He completed the work for us, leaving no room for pride and boasting in the Christian life. But not only this, God has already mapped out our path to greatness. He has already gone ahead of us and prepared good works for us to do. Our job is to step into that calling. So, what exactly is your calling? Who better to ask than the One who has prepared it? I love to ask God questions in prayer and then just wait in silence for His response.

For most of my journey with Jesus, I have served people through a variety of ways—except for one year. I was in college. Well, sort of. I had just been kicked out of Bible college after they realized that in two years of taking a completely full schedule, including summer and winter courses, living on campus with a meal plan, and purchasing every textbook, sweatshirt, pen, and coffee cup, I had simply been saying "Just put it on my tab." Somehow, I flew under the radar and was already over halfway to a bachelor's degree when a sweet old lady interrupted my professor's lecture on hermeneutics (how to study the Bible) and pulled me out of class. She sat me down in a business office and swung a computer monitor around so we could both stare at an archaic looking spreadsheet with a black background and a white jumble of numbers and letters overwhelming the screen and my senses. She pointed to a corner of the screen, and almost breathless she cut to the chase: "You have been attending here for almost two whole years, and you haven't paid us a dime!" To which I responded, "Yeah. I don't have any money." And then we just stared at each other in silence. That day we both decided I could no longer afford a private Christian college.

In need of a place to live, I packed up my tan Nissan Altima with my belongings and drove to Oregon to live with my mom. I would work, hunt, fish, hike, and enjoy life while I figured out my next move with academia. When I left Arizona, I left behind my life of serving others to focus more on me. I didn't volunteer at church, I didn't work with kids or youth, I didn't even think about the homeless or the hurting I had to walk around to get into the coffee shop I worked at. I just thought about me. Every day I was surrounded by the beauty of creation. I had good food. I was in a great, loving home. I had freedom to explore and try new things. And each day I slowly became more miserable than the day before. Anticipation crept into depression. I had wandered off the path of greatness God had for me, and my soul knew it long before my mind did. I was only serving myself, which goes completely against the grain of God's design for us, and my world was imploding.

Joy in Serving

For some reason we convince ourselves that serving others is a burden that will rob us of joy. Do you know who doesn't think that way? People who are serving within the gifting and calling that God has given them. Of course, we can run the risk of doing too much and burning ourselves out (more about this in chapter 9), but when we focus on others and find a rhythm of doing the good work that God has prepared for us, it is life-giving. I had the privilege of interviewing one of our oldest church members, Rosa, who lived to be 103 years old. She was close to 100 when I sat with her, and although mobility had limited her ability to serve in the ways that she used to, it hadn't eliminated it completely. She told me, "Each morning I wake up and say, 'Lord, what work do you have for me to do today?' And whatever it is, I do that." Even at 100 years old, Rosa quilted, stitching in Bible verses for use in hospitals, sewed puppets for Sunday school teachers, and crafted walnut shells with a tiny felt-fabric baby Jesus inside. She called them "the gospel in a nutshell" and would use them to share Jesus with anyone she encountered. When she no longer had the ability to craft, her new assignment was to pray and encourage her fellow seniors at the assisted care facility where she had started a Bible study. "Jesus still hasn't called me home, so there must be more work to be done. But I'm ready," she said with a warm smile.

There are two types of people in the world: thinkers and feelers. If you aren't sure which one you are, you are an overthinker. Don't overthink serving. It's what we were created for, and it's the definition of greatness. Just start somewhere, even if it is simple. If you're waiting for the perfect plan, the perfect opportunity, or the right invitation, it's possible you will never begin. I have learned that the best way to find the work God has prepared for me is to take a step. I don't know where the path will lead, but God reveals it as I walk with Him one step at a time. The further I walk, the clearer I understand what He has prepared for me to do. He may surprise me from time to time, but the work always seems to bless me even more than it blesses others. I want that joy for you.

QUESTIONS FOR REFLECTION AND DISCUSSION

What is greatness?

What are the differences between greatness according to God and greatness according to the world?

Have you ever experienced joy in serving others? What was it you were doing?

What is one thing you can do daily or weekly to serve others?

[8]

Simple Finances

Command them to do good, to be rich in good deeds, and to be generous and willing to share. In this way they will lay up treasure for themselves as a firm foundation for the coming age, so that they may take hold of the life that is truly life.

1 Timothy 6:18–19

The happiest people I know are also some of the most generous people I know. And that is not just one person's observation. Take a moment right now to think of the happiest people you have ever encountered in your lifetime. I am confident that most, if not all, are marked by generosity. Even from a secular perspective, you cannot deny this reality. Dr. Summer Allen, in her paper "The Science of Generosity," cites hundreds of studies that demonstrate generosity is directly linked to longer life, relational satisfaction and intimacy, overall happiness, and health.[1] This doesn't seem to add up in an age dominated by the secular Darwinian worldview characterized by the survival of the fittest. If this is true, why is giving not only beneficial to the receiver but also to the giver? It's rather simple: because that is how God designed it. In this chapter, we will examine God's design for stewarding our income.

A Central Topic of Faith

At one point during His short public ministry, Jesus delivered a sermon that explored the ways the kingdom of heaven impacts life on earth (Matt. 5–7). As you read through the "Sermon on the Mount," note how often Jesus speaks about money and generosity. In this short sermon that takes only about fifteen minutes to read, Jesus mentions this topic seven times.[2] In Jewish writing and teaching, when something is repeated it means it is very important. If something is repeated seven times, it is absolutely paramount.

Why does money have such bearing on our lives? Perhaps it's because it promises many of the same things that Jesus promises us. For example, money promises to take care of us and to give us security, significance, fulfillment, peace, and joy. We chase after it and convince ourselves repeatedly that we will be satisfied once we obtain it. The only problem is this is a lie. Have you ever known somebody who was rich and miserable? Maybe not from a distance, but when you really started to get to know them, you discovered money's little secret: It's no savior at all. You can be successful in business and fail at life. You can be financially wealthy and relationally poor. You can climb all the way to the top and realize it was the wrong mountain. Or you can choose to trust Jesus. The sooner we can learn to trust the ways of Jesus when it comes to money, the more abundant our life will be.

God's Design for Finances

It's helpful to remember that we are stewarding what God has given us; we don't get to keep it. Just as we came into this world with nothing, we don't get to take anything out of this world with us other than our relationships and experiences. Jesus regularly redirects our mindset to think in terms of steward-ship, not ownership. Moses writes, "You may say to yourself, 'My power and the strength of my hands have produced this wealth for me.' But remember the LORD your God, for it is he who gives you the ability to produce wealth, and so con-firms his covenant, which he swore to your ancestors, as it is today" (Deut. 8:17–18). Our ability and opportunity to work and build wealth come from God. We are stewards of the opportunity and the resulting income God gifts each of us.

Solomon, one of the wisest and wealthiest people ever to live, wrote often about finances in his collection of wisdom known as the book of Proverbs. If we were to consolidate all his writings along with other teachings found throughout the Bible, we would arrive at the principles regularly taught at the church where I pastor. When we receive income, we follow three steps: First, we give; second, we save; and third, we live on the remainder. Give, save, live. It's that simple. Giving first honors God, saving second builds wealth, and living on the rest teaches us contentment.

Give First

Honor the LORD with your wealth, with the *firstfruits* of all your crops. (Prov. 3:9)

Our natural tendency is to give last, but the Bible teaches us to give first. Why? Giving first shows honor to God and acknowledges that He is the source of every resource. The Bible also instructs us to give a percentage of our income. The biblical word "tithe" means ten percent. It dates all the way back to the time of Abraham. In the book of Genesis, God assists Abram (later called Abraham) in defeating the forces of multiple kingdoms (Gen. 13–14). These kingdoms had stolen Abram's possessions along with many of the people who were with him. Then a mysterious figure known as Melchizedek, a priest of God, arrives with bread and wine. Melchizedek—a foreshadowing of Jesus, our great High Priest—blesses Abram, and Abram gives a tenth of everything he has as an offering. We see this principle again in Genesis 28 when Jacob, Abraham's grandson, acknowledges God's provision in his life and vows to give a tenth of all he has. As the Old Testament progresses, tithing would become established as a requirement.

When Jesus established the new covenant of grace, the old covenant of the law was fulfilled and finished. There is no New Testament obligation to give ten percent. We are clearly instructed to give freely, cheerfully, and generously whatever we have decided in our hearts to give. I believe that because tithing is modeled before the giving of the Old Testament law, it should be our goal. Percentage giving is mentioned by Paul to both the Galatian church and Corinthian church when he tells them: "On the first day of every week, each one of you should set aside a sum of money in keeping with your income, saving it up" (1 Cor. 16:1–2). This means we give in proportion to what we make, or in other words, a percentage. If 10 percent seems scary to you, ask yourself, What can I trust God with today? If it is 2 percent, start there. It is a good practice that whenever you receive income, you think to give first. And God's challenge would be for us to increase our giving as time goes on. This is the great paradox of generosity: Giving gives to the giver. As Jesus said, "It is more blessed to give than to receive" (Acts 20:35).

Save Second

The wise store up choice food and olive oil, but fools gulp theirs down. (Prov. 21:20)

What if I told you that wealth isn't a bad thing? It seems controversial, right? Well, contrary to what many expect, the Bible doesn't teach that wealth is bad. In fact, the principles of the Bible regularly practiced will build wealth over time. Those who teach that all wealth is bad will often misquote 1 Timothy 6, saying, "Money is the root of all evil." What Paul actually says to Timothy is "the love of money is a root of all kinds of evil" (v. 10). Wealth isn't bad, but the worship of it is. You can be wealthy and follow Jesus. You can also be poor and follow Jesus. And just to be clear, odds are, if you are reading or listening to this book, you are rich. As of the writing of this book, according to Macrotrends, if your household income is higher than $12,688 a year, you are living with the richer half of humanity, even though it might not feel that way.[3] One of the reasons it doesn't feel that way is because most people live paycheck to paycheck.

Early in our marriage, my wife and I did two of the three biblical steps when it came to our income. We gave and we lived.

When one of us would get a raise, we'd celebrate and eat a little fancier. As our income crept up, so did our lifestyle. Then in 2007 we made a life-changing decision to go down to one income and start a family together. This felt impossible, and it was, if we were going to keep practicing our old habits. We signed up for a financial class that taught us the biblical principles of give, save, and live. We started implementing these principles right away. For me, saving was the most difficult of the three. We created a monthly budget and, like we did with giving, we made saving ten percent a top priority. Saving is another form of loving and giving to another person. That person just happens to be the future you. In the famous marshmallow experiment, kids often opted for the single marshmallow in front of them over the promised double portion later. It's in our nature. Which is why we need to be taught to operate under God's future-thinking principles. Now that I am a little older, I am so grateful for our younger selves trusting God's guidance and creating a discipline of saving. It has helped us build wealth over time and has simultaneously put us in a position to grow in generosity.

Live on the Rest

A heart at peace gives life to the body, but envy rots the bones. (Prov. 14:30)

Oil tycoon John D. Rockefeller was the wealthiest person on the planet when he was asked by a reporter, "How much money is enough?" Rockefeller, without hesitation, responded, "Just a little bit more."[4] Our insatiable longing for just a little bit more threatens our ability to give and to save. God wants so much more for us. He wants us to have a heart at peace, content with what we have.

This is a difficult task in our current time. We live in a culture fueled by envy. Businesses buy, sell, and trade our attention to convince us that whatever they have to offer will bring us long-awaited happiness. Lifestyles of the rich and famous are constantly on display in all forms of media, causing us to swoon over the thought of an indoor swimming pool, a private chef, a dream vacation, and a fancy car. Every day we are fed the fuel of discontentment. If past generations could get a glimpse of what we have available to us today—cell phones, clean water, cars, air conditioning, antibiotics, Amazon, and a life expectancy almost double what it was in 1800—they would expect to find a generation overflowing with contentment. Instead, they would find the opposite to be true. So how is it possible that we have so much more yet feel it so much less? Because "enough" is a moving target.

Paul writes the following words to Timothy, a young pastor who is dealing with those who are constantly chasing more earthly possessions: "But godliness with contentment is great gain. For we brought nothing into the world, and we can take nothing out of it. But if we have food and clothing, we will be content with that" (1 Tim. 6:6–8). How free would we be if our level of "enough" was food and clothing? God wants that for us. He wants everything beyond our basic needs to be a cause for gratitude and celebration. Contentment doesn't come from spending more; contentment comes from wanting less.

Learning the practice of give, save, and live honors God, builds wealth, and teaches contentment. Budgeting and operating within these principles will free you from the yoke of financial slavery and open the door for God's blessings to flow through your life.

QUESTIONS FOR REFLECTION AND DISCUSSION

Which one of the three financial practices (give, save, live) is the most challenging for you? Why do you think that is?

What possessions would you consider to be necessary for contentment?

Do you think being wealthy is a bad thing or a good thing? When do you think our desire for more might cross a line into being a trap?

Why do you think Jesus talked about money as one of God's chief competitors for our hearts?

Jesus said, "It is more blessed to give than to receive" (Acts 20:35). How have you personally experienced that?

[9]

Simple Rhythms

Come to me, all you who are weary and burdened, and
I will give you rest. Take my yoke upon you and learn
from me, for I am gentle and humble in heart, and you
will find rest for your souls. For my yoke is easy and my
burden is light.

Matthew 11:28–30

In this chapter, we will learn about a rhythm God has created
and modeled for us to live by. God invites us into intentional
weekly rest known as "Sabbath" to slow our pace and experience freedom from the tyranny of busyness.

The more we discover about God's creation, the more we realize nothing is static in the universe. Everything is in motion.

Even rocks are alive with a frantic dance of energy and particles at a subatomic level. Our lives are constantly in motion, and yet we often seek after the elusive myth of balance. To me, balance implies walking a tightrope in which the slightest shift could easily lead to a catastrophic plummet. If you were to balance sound, you would have a monotone hum akin to the sound of a heart monitor at the time of death. Balance is unmoving, still, and lifeless. Trying to find balance is more burdensome than it is realistic. I prefer the term rhythm.

Rhythm is what you see in life. Rhythm implies motion, music, and life. When we observe God's creation, we see rhythms everywhere. We see rhythms in heartbeats, seasons, animals, tides, relationships, cells, atoms, and the cosmos. In his book *Mere Christianity*, C. S. Lewis articulates, "God is not a static thing—not even a person—but a dynamic, pulsating activity, a life, almost a kind of drama. Almost, if you will not think me irreverent, a kind of dance"[1] between the Father, Son, and Holy Spirit. Just as God is not static, neither is His creation; it is constantly in motion. And woven throughout the dance of creation are patterns of starts and stops.

A Divine Invitation

In Matthew 11:28–30, Jesus invites all of us who are weary and burdened to take His yoke upon us. I believe all of us regularly fall into the weary and burdened category, which means all of us are invited to share the yoke of Jesus. A yoke is a large piece of wood that connects two oxen together. This simple illustration captures Jesus's invitation to us: "Let Me come beside you and walk with you." I like to picture Jesus putting His arm around me and walking beside me, step for step. Eugene Peterson beautifully paraphrases Jesus's words, "Walk with me and work with me—watch how I do it. Learn the unforced rhythms of grace" (Matt. 11:29 MSG). What are the rhythms of grace that Jesus taught and modeled? Let's start at the very beginning.

After God created the heavens and the earth and everything within them, He did something unexpected: He rested (Gen. 2:1–2). The infinitely powerful God did not rest because He was tired; He rested because that was His rhythm for Himself and for His creation (v. 3). God blessed one day of the week and called it "holy," meaning "set apart." Included within the Ten Commandments God gave to Moses was the command to set apart one day a week for rest. The Hebrew word for this day is *shabbat* from which we get the word "Sabbath." It means "to cease." For the Israelites, this marked a new way of life. Having only known bondage in Egypt, where slaves never had a day off, they were now learning to live in freedom.

Life Found in Rest

Dan Buettner, a researcher on life expectancy and longevity, found a group of people who live, on average, ten years longer than everyone else. This group, known as Seventh-day Adventists, are best known for their strict observance of the Sabbath. Buettner explains, "They take this idea of Sabbath very seriously, so they're decompressing their stress. About 84% of health care dollars are spent because of bad food choices, inactivity, and unmanaged stress, and they have these cultural ways of managing stress through their Sabbath."[2] Not only do they gain ten years at the end of their lives, but they also gain another ten along the way when you add up all the days that they observed the Sabbath. They've learned the practice of being a human *being*, not a human *doing*. They have learned to pause and be fully present with God, to glorify Him by enjoying life. For us to experience this, we must enter God's sacred rhythms. In response to a question about how to maintain spiritual health, Dallas Willard, a renowned author on spiritual formation, responded, "You must ruthlessly eliminate hurry from your life."[3] The unhurried way was the way of Jesus.

This is not to say that this will come easy to us. Like the Israelites, we may need to learn how to live in freedom. I'm well aware that taking a day of rest each week might feel overwhelming with all that we have going on. But this is why it is an act of faith. Like trusting God with our finances by giving first, we trust God with our time by setting aside a day dedicated to Him. It may seem counterintuitive, but you will gain more from giving up this time than by filling it with the busyness of your weekly schedule. In yet another case of science catching up with Scripture, studies now confirm that life is designed to operate around set rhythms of work and rest. One study conducted by Stanford University found that productivity significantly decreases after working more than fifty hours per week, and there is almost no difference whether working fifty-five or seventy hours.[4]

Jesus modeled rest. In one of my favorite accounts in the book of Matthew, Jesus and His disciples are in a boat on the sea of Galilee. Soon they encounter a fierce storm. While the storm rages and threatens to capsize them, Jesus remains fast asleep. His disciples on the other hand are fighting for their lives. Why would Jesus be sleeping during a storm? Because He was tired. His disciples woke Him up and were amazed when He simply hushed the storm. Matthew doesn't elaborate, but I like to think Jesus went back to sleep. Sometimes the most spiritual thing you can do is to go take a nap. Our leader modeled that for us.

When I ask people how things are going, I almost always get the same answer: "Busy." When people ask me how things are going, I often have the same response. We exist in a very time-impoverished era. It's in our nature to push our limits. However, when we do this, we suffer, those around us suffer, and our relationship with God suffers. It's impossible to spend quality time in a hurry. Sabbath is like a built-in brake pedal to keep us from careening out of control. For followers of Jesus, the practice of Sabbath rest is more than just a day off work; it's an intentional and thoughtful act of worship. It's remembering the work that God has done in creation and the work He is doing in our re-creation and then pausing to enjoy it with Him. It's designed to be a refueling time physically, relationally, and spiritually.

Intentionality

Depending on your job and your schedule, your Sabbath might look a little different. For instance, as a pastor, I work on Sundays, so Friday is my Sabbath day. If your work schedule rotates, rotate your Sabbath. But this day should be different from the other days. I believe, as modeled by the early church, the Sabbath should include corporate worship with your local church (if you can Sabbath on weekends). It should include being physically energized with good food and perhaps some form of activity. If you refuel by being outside, go for a walk or a hike, sit at a park, or go fishing. If you refuel in solitude, meditate on a verse of the Bible or spend time reading a book.

Listen to music. Paint. God created you unique, and you may refuel in different ways than others. That is okay. Use this day to spend extended time with the most important people in your life. You may even consider taking a break from your phone or television. Talk with God. Thank Him for this holy day and consider asking Him how He wants you to enjoy it. And then rest in it. And rest in the reality that God loves you and has given this day as a gift to you.

In addition to our weekly Sabbath, we see another daily rhythm modeled by Jesus: setting aside time to be with God. In the first chapter of Mark's Gospel, he notes the launch of Jesus's public ministry and His immediate popularity among the people. During Jesus's first day in the town of Capernaum, He taught in the synagogue, cast out a demon, and healed Peter's mother-in-law. By evening, the entire town showed up with their sick and demon-possessed. From this moment forward, we might assume that Jesus would be too busy for anything else. But Mark observes that on the second day of Jesus's public ministry, He found time to pray: "Very early in the morning, while it was still dark, Jesus got up, left the house and went off to a solitary place, where he prayed" (Mark 1:35).

We don't know every detail of everything Jesus did, but we do know that praying was one thing He consistently did. This was Jesus's routine. Even the disciples were shocked by it. When they woke up to find that Jesus was missing, "Simon and his companions went to look for him, and when they found him, they exclaimed: 'Everyone is looking for you!'" (vv. 36–37). We can feel the gravity of this moment in the disciples' exclamation. So what does Jesus do in response? He tells them, "'Let us go somewhere else—to the nearby villages—so I can preach there also. That is why I have come'" (v. 38). In a sense, Jesus says "no" to hurry. He refuses to be controlled by the tyranny of the urgent.

Learning to Say No

Saying no is not just a good idea; it's a mathematical necessity. Time is our most valuable resource, and we only get a limited amount of it. Once we spend what we have, it's gone forever. There will always be more demands for our time than there is time to give. If you are anything like me, then saying no can be a challenge because you don't want to disappoint people. Jesus was okay with disappointing people to keep His priorities. To follow His example, we need to know what our priorities are, and our calendars need to reflect them. I once heard a pastor say that our calendar is our second most sacred document next to our Bible. Our Bible is where we get our instruction from God; our calendar is often where we set aside the time to apply it. Setting aside intentional time is vital to the health of our soul and our relationships with others.

Even with a carefully planned schedule, it's possible that the most important thing in your day is not even on your agenda. In the words of German theologian Dietrich Bonhoeffer, "We must be ready to allow ourselves to be interrupted by God. God will be constantly crossing our paths and canceling our plans by sending us people with claims and petitions. . . . We do not assume that our schedule is our own to manage, but allow it to be arranged by God."[5] Leaving space in our schedules is an open invitation for God to work through us in unexpected ways. God wants to love people through us, but that rarely happens when we are in a hurry. I'm amazed when I look back and think of the moments God used people to make a positive impact on my life. They weren't preset appointments. They were unexpected moments with people who were simply available. When we allow God to work through our schedules, we move from spending our time to investing our time in what matters most.

QUESTIONS FOR REFLECTION AND DISCUSSION

How does Jesus teach us to pace our lives?

If you were to think of your soul like a battery, what charge percentage would you say you were at right now (0 being empty and 100 being completely full)?

How does Jesus teach us to recharge when we are feeling burnt out and weary?

How does our calendar reveal what our top priorities are?

What are some changes you would like to make to your schedule moving forward in light of what you just read?

[10]

Simple Worship

Let the message of Christ dwell among you richly as you teach and admonish one another with all wisdom through psalms, hymns, and songs from the Spirit, singing to God with gratitude in your hearts.

Colossians 3:16

Everybody worships something. It's in our nature. It may be sports, music, nature, movies, appearance, money, strength, sex, power, people, and even our pets. In this chapter, we will define worship and learn how to properly channel our worship to the One who is worthy of it.

When I was barely old enough to walk, I worshiped Superman. Minus his mild intolerance to kryptonite, what wasn't there to love about Superman?! I thought about him constantly. I watched his movies. I read comics about him. I even pretended to be him, wearing homemade blue onesie pajamas with red underwear pulled up over them and a blanket for a cape with a crudely drawn "S" taped to it. When, at the age of two, we moved to a new neighborhood, it was months before my neighbors learned that my name was Robert. Whenever they would ask me my name, I would confidently declare, "I'm Superman!" I had recurring dreams of flying. Confident it wasn't just a dream, I jumped from stairs, fences, and trees using grocery bags as backup parachutes. After each attempt, I convinced myself that just for a moment, I flew. As I got older, I outgrew wearing underwear over my clothes, but I remained secretly enamored with Superman, even as I entered elementary school. I drew my own comics and created my own storylines. I was devastated the day I read the comic *Superman #75*, "The Death of Superman," created to boost weakening comic book sales—and crush ten-year-old hearts. If you think back on your life, I'm sure there have been things you have worshiped too.

Biblical worship is about turning our attention and affection in God's direction. It's about orienting our worshiping nature to the One who truly deserves it. He is the Author of everything, including the very things we are so prone to worship. To worship anything else is to worship the creation rather than the Creator.

Worship Defined

Theologian A. W. Pink defines biblical worship as "a redeemed heart, occupied with God, expressing itself in adoration and thanksgiving."[1] There are lots of ways we can do this. One way is through music. If you are new to the faith and find it strange that people in church sing songs together, you aren't the first. You've probably only experienced community singing at birthdays, during the seventh-inning stretch, or at a concert. Singing is older than time because God sings. Zephaniah records that God "will rejoice over you with singing" (Zeph. 3:17). Our affinity for music reflects our Creator. What better way to worship than to reflect His gift back to Him. The people of Israel have the honor of singing the first song in the Bible known as the "Song of Moses and Miriam." This song praises God for His miraculous deliverance from the Egyptian army by parting the sea and then collapsing it back on their pursuers. The song begins, "I will sing to the LORD, for he is highly exalted. Both horse and driver he has hurled into the sea. The LORD is my strength and my defense; he has become my salvation. He is my God, and I will praise him, my father's God, and I will exalt him" (Exod. 15:1–2). God's people have been singing songs together ever since. The book of Psalms (the longest book in the Bible) is a collection of songs for various occasions. In the New Testament, we find Jesus and His disciples singing together after the Last Supper (Matt. 26:30). The apostle Paul instructs the churches at Ephesus and Colossae to sing "psalms, hymns, and spiritual songs" together, a practice that continues to this day (Eph. 5:19; Col. 3:16).

More Than Just Music

God designed worship to do more than simply glorify Himself; He designed it to transform the worshiper. Have you ever had a song stuck in your head? It happens to me all the time, sometimes even in the middle of the night. The *Time* magazine article "Why We Remember Music and Forget Everything Else" explains the power of music for the human brain.[2] The article says that even when nonmusicians listen to music, it activates reward mechanisms within their brains, releasing endorphins and capturing both the contents and the emotions conveyed in the song. In other words, music has the power to connect far deeper than words alone. Music allows us to have an experience with God, from God, and with one another. Truth and Scripture put to music remain with us well beyond the experience, flooding our subconscious and transforming our minds. If we are to love God with all our heart, soul, mind, and strength, then music is the perfect conduit.

Worship extends far beyond just music. We can express our adoration and gratitude in several different ways. Earlier in this book, we talked about prayer. Prayer is an act of worship. Studying God's Word is worship. Enjoying the gifts we have in this life with gratitude toward the Giver of the gifts is an act of worship. Serving others is an act of worship. To create space for God and people in our schedules, to give of our income, to practice the principles of following Jesus—these are all acts of worship. Paul writes to the church in Rome, "In view of God's mercy, . . . offer your bodies as a living sacrifice, holy and pleasing to God—this is your true and proper worship" (Rom. 12:1). We can offer our bodies as "a living sacrifice" because Jesus was the final sacrifice in the history of the sacrificial system. The author of Hebrews explains that under the old sacrificial system the priests had to offer constant sacrifices to cover the constant sins of the people (Heb. 10:11). This work was completed by Jesus: "For by one sacrifice he has made perfect forever those who are being made holy" (v. 14). The word "redeem" means to "buy back." We were lost to sin and death when Jesus bought us back at a price: His life for ours. Until we put our faith in the work, atonement, and leadership of Jesus, our singing and serving is not biblical worship. Once we have been made alive in Christ by His grace through faith, we can choose to offer our lives—not as a dead sacrifice but a living one—in service to the King.

Gratitude

Giving our full attention to God is never easy. It is something that grows ever more challenging as new technology captures our thoughts and consumes our time. One way we can reorient our attention to God is through prayer. Look around you right now. What is one thing you can thank God for? One of my favorite prayers is to simply say, "Thank You, Jesus." If we look for them, we will find opportunities every single day to say, "Thank You, Jesus." Paul writes to the church in Thessalonica: "Rejoice always, pray continually, give thanks in all circumstances; for this is God's will for you in Christ Jesus" (1 Thess. 5:16–18). To pray continually is to operate with an awareness of the Holy Spirit's presence with you wherever you go. It is to be occupied by God and to look for opportunities to praise Him, serve Him, listen to Him, or just simply be with Him. I recently heard of something called "Red Car Theory" used as a business analogy for spotting opportunities.[3] I believe we can apply it differently here. Odds are, if I were to ask you after a day of work, school, or running errands, "How many red cars did you see on the road today?" your response would likely be along the lines of, "I don't know. I wasn't paying any attention." If I then offered you fifty dollars for every red car you saw the next day, you would know close to the exact number. So how did you go from seeing nothing to seeing everything? You were motivated to start looking. One of our responses to the incredible work God has done in our lives is to be motivated to look for opportunities to be grateful and praise Him. All around you are reasons to praise God if you just start looking.

Focus

In his formative book *Celebration of Discipline*, Richard Foster breaks down the variety of spiritual disciplines into three main categories: *inward* (prayer, meditation, study, and fasting), *outward* (solitude, simplicity, submission, and service), and *corporate* (celebration, musical worship, confession, and guidance).[4] These practices together fuel what I believe is the key to worship: focus. Fasting, the age-old practice of replacing food or other regular routines with prayer, focuses our attention. Solitude eliminates the constant noise surrounding us, allowing us to focus. Gathering in church services for worship, the Word, and waiting on the Holy Spirit turns our hearts and souls toward God with greater focus. Whatever you focus on is what you move toward.

Worship involves focusing our attention. When we direct our focus toward God, we draw closer to Him. Our natural inclination is to center our attention on ourselves. However, as we shift our focus to God, our self-centeredness diminishes. Rick Warren brilliantly states, "Humility is not thinking less of yourself, but thinking of yourself less."[5] A preoccupation with ourselves leads to selfishness, bitterness, lack of control, and more. In contrast, a redeemed heart expressing adoration and thanksgiving to God, leads to "love, joy, peace, patience, kindness, goodness, faithfulness, gentleness, and self-control" (Gal. 5:22–23 NLT).

QUESTIONS FOR REFLECTION AND DISCUSSION

How does music help us worship God?

What does God's creation of music tell you about Him?

What are ways, other than music, that we worship God?

What do you think would happen if we thought less about ourselves and more about God?

What is one thing, right now, you are very grateful for?

PART 3

SIMPLE RELATIONSHIPS

[11]

Simple Marriage

"'For this reason a man will leave his father and mother and be united to his wife, and the two will become one flesh.' So they are no longer two, but one flesh. Therefore what God has joined together, let no one separate."

Mark 10:7–9

Marriage is simple, but by no means is it easy. It's an incredible gift, but it can easily be distorted. In this chapter, we will go back to the beginning to understand God's design behind marriage. We will then learn from the example of Jesus and the writings of Paul the best practices for a healthy, lifelong marriage.

Our Story

Lindsay and I met while we were both still in college. While my college experience was more of an "escape the room" challenge, bouncing between universities and majors, Lindsay's was more straightforward. She was an intern at the church I attended, and despite not knowing each other, we both signed up for the same mission trip to Africa. We met briefly for a couple trainings, but we didn't talk much. I was new to the group and a little intimidated by this socially connected, beautiful, confident young woman, and so I decided to focus on building friendships with the guys and experience the excitement of serving and exploring a foreign land. To both of our surprise, we were seated next to each other on the plane. This was before the time of personal video screens and noise-canceling headphones, so we were forced to engage in something neither of us was overly interested in: talking. It took around twenty hours to travel by plane from Phoenix to Morocco, with a layover in Europe. This duration was longer than our previous conversations, which had lasted only minutes. As I listened to her stories, learned about her life, and glimpsed into her heart, something began to stir within me.

Morocco is an Islamic country, and when we landed this became apparent. As soon as we were off the plane, men and women were required to remain separate. Because of this, Lindsay and I didn't see much of each other for most of the trip except for during occasional team debriefs. For one part of the trip, we served together at an orphanage, painting murals and playing with the kids. She was amazing. The love of Jesus flowed through her to the children and to everyone she encountered. *She's so beautiful*, I thought to myself. *Am*

I staring? I'm staring. Stop staring. Before each of the flights home, I casually glanced at her ticket. The Lord had shown favor upon me once again! Eager to get to know her, this time I didn't hesitate to start asking deeper questions. Sixteen hours into our flight, sleep-deprived and rapidly approaching our destination, I said to her, "I think I have the answer to all of our problems." In response, she looked at me, confused. Then I tried a line that sounded so right in my head: "You and I just need to fall madly in love with each other." If you're thinking that I am embellishing this story, I wish you were right. I had just used the worst line to try to woo Lindsay, and she responded with . . . silence. Painful, awkward, deafening silence. Reacting quickly, I said, "Just kidding." *Whew. Quick thinking, Robert! You really bailed yourself out.* After this, we continued to hang out as friends and eventually we started dating. Within a year we were married. Now, three kids and two decades later, we are more in love than we have ever been. I want what we have for every marriage. It's amazing, but at the same time, it's delicate and requires protection.

God's Design for Marriage

Marriage is a sacred gift, and it dates all the way back to the beginning. In the book of Genesis, after God created everything except for humankind, he arrived at the crescendo of creation. God, who is one essence with three distinct persons, says, "'Let *us* make mankind in *our* image, in *our* likeness, so that they may rule over the fish in the sea and the birds in the sky, over the livestock and all the wild animals, and over all the creatures that move along the ground.' So God created mankind in his own image, in the image of God he created them; male and female he created them" (Gen. 1:26–27). In the next chapter, we learn that the first thing that wasn't good in creation was for man to be alone (Gen. 2:18). God, who in His very nature is relational, wanted more for humanity. So He took a rib from the side of Adam and created Eve. It was the first ever sacred joining of male and female. Adam bursts into poetry over this miracle of one flesh being made into two and of two becoming one. Jesus quotes Genesis 2:24 as He reinforces the sanctity of marriage: "'For this reason a man will leave his father and mother and be united to his wife, and the two will become one flesh.' So they are no longer two, but one flesh. Therefore what God has joined together, let no one separate" (Mark 10:7–9).

God takes His promises seriously, and our relationship with Him is built on them. God designed marriage to be built on a promise: the promise to keep the "one flesh" *one*. If you are reading this and have been through a divorce or have had sex before marriage, know that God doesn't want to shame you, and neither do I. Even when we miss the mark on His intended design, He doesn't abandon us. If that were the case, we'd all be helpless. But He does want the best for you. And the best gifts are experienced within their intended design. As you move forward in faith, trust God and experience the gift as He has intended it for you.

Backward Culture

We live in a culture that reverses the order of God's design. Dating apps are designed to emphasize physical attractiveness. Our culture celebrates expressing ourselves sexually after only a few dates as part of the early stages of connection. The couple might discuss faith and religion, but in many ways, this is becoming less common. Often, it's not until they begin raising children that conversations around faith and church become more relevant. Couples will move in together to try out what it might be like to be married, and if it lasts long enough, they might even throw together a wedding party and make it official. But that isn't how God's design works. God's design begins with respect for the sacred gift of marriage and sexuality. Faith, friendship, attraction, commitment, marriage, and sexuality are the designed path for full enjoyment of God's good gift. Friendship is a stronger foundation than mere physical attraction.

For those who are single, Paul, who was also not married, celebrates the benefits that come from undivided attention to the Lord (1 Cor. 7:7–8, 38). Not everyone should marry. If you are single and desire to be married one day, my advice would be to focus first on your relationship with Jesus and allow the Holy Spirit to do the work of transformation discussed in this book. Marriage doesn't solve problems and, in fact, often magnifies our unresolved issues from our singleness. Those who are emotionally, relationally, and spiritually healthy in singleness are those who are healthiest in marriage.

Foundational Faith

The importance of faith in relationships is understated. I don't know of any couples that marry in hopes of one day getting a divorce. We all desire to stay married. And yet today, half of all marriages end in divorce, and an even higher percentage of second marriages fail.[1] Relationships built on a foundation of faith are better equipped to weather the storms. Couples that attend church together, attend a small group, or pray together have lower percentages of divorce and higher marital satisfaction.[2] There are supernatural benefits to allowing the Author of relationships to be the authority in our marriages. There are also natural benefits of practices such as prayer woven into our relational design. Brad Wilcox from the Institute for Family Studies explains that "[the practice of] prayer helps couples deal with stress, enables them to focus on shared beliefs and hopes for the future, and allows them to deal constructively with challenges and problems in their relationship, and in their lives. In fact, we find that shared prayer is the most powerful religious predictor of relationship quality."[3] This is why, before you start dating, you want to be certain there is a genuine faith component in your potential boyfriend or girlfriend. If you are reading this and are already married but your spouse is not a follower of Jesus, then choose to pray for them daily and model the principles outlined in this book. With the power of the Holy Spirit and the love of Jesus flowing unconditionally through you, there is a strong possibility they will be drawn into the wonderful life of faith.

Jesus and the Church

In Ephesians 5, the apostle Paul points to the picture of Jesus and the church as the model for marriage. Like Jesus's love for the church, marriage is a relationship of self-sacrificing love and respect. Wives are called to honor and respect their husbands. Practically speaking, this does not mean that they must tolerate an overbearing or even abusive husband, nor does it imply that wives are inferior. Many husbands manipulate this passage as an excuse to "lord over their wives." Jesus clearly speaks against this line of thinking. For wives, the call to respect and honor your husband means not talking negatively about him when he isn't around. This is an all-too-common practice for both husbands and wives, and it's cancerous to marriage, ultimately pushing spouses apart rather than bringing them closer together. If you are a husband out with the guys or a wife out with the ladies, choose to refrain when the conversation turns to all the things people can't stand about their spouses. It not only dishonors their spouses, but it will also begin to poison them as well. If there is an issue with your spouse, talk *with* them rather than *about* them (more on this in chapter 15).

Having given instruction to wives, Paul then turns his attention to husbands, calling on them to love their wives just as Christ loved the church. In the ancient Greek language, there are four words that can be used for "love." *Eros* is the word used for physical love, from which we get the word "erotic." *Storge* is the word for a familial parental love, like the love a parent has for their child. *Philia* means brotherly love or a love between friends. However, Paul does not use any of these words but instead opts for the fourth word, *agape*, which means unconditional, self-sacrificing love. In other words, it's the type of love that God demonstrated to us through His Son, Jesus. Paul then illustrates this with a snapshot of a time shortly before Jesus went to the cross, when all authority had been given to Him, and He humbly wrapped a towel around His waist and began washing the feet of His disciples. Husbands, this is to be our posture toward our wives. It means being willing to sacrifice everything, even our lives, for our spouses. When we submit ourselves to self-sacrificing love and respect for one another, we put the message of the gospel on display to the world.

Intentionally Grateful

Ongoing gratitude is key to growing a thriving marriage. This is where the Red Car Theory comes in handy again. If you recall, the theory says that you will find what you are looking for if you are motivated to look. If you are looking for things to be unhappy about in your marriage, you will spot them. I can promise this because you married a sinner and so did your spouse. If you are looking for things to be grateful for in your marriage, you will spot them too. When Lindsay and I were engaged, we met regularly with my grandparents for counseling. We were given the assignment of writing down twenty-five things we love about the other person. The next week, we were given the assignment again. By our next session, we had to come up with twenty-five more things with no repeats. The next week—you guessed it—another twenty-five. And so on. Let me tell you, there comes a point in that process where you get writer's block. But then, just when you think you can't come up with anything else, you find yourself looking at new categories from new angles and the compliments begin to flow again. At week six, we were released from the assignment, but we had unleashed a new practice. We learned to see the "red cars."

One practice I recommend to engaged couples is to compliment the other person daily. This leads to multiple benefits within marriage. First, it's honoring and loving, which increases intimacy. Second, it increases your appreciation for your spouse or future spouse. Third, it reinforces their positive qualities. Some couples mistakenly believe that calling out and correcting minor behaviors will strengthen their relationship. The book of Proverbs equates that to having "a leaky roof in a rainstorm" (27:15). Positive reinforcement is a powerful tool in marriage. Whatever gets rewarded gets repeated.

Couples that stop looking for the positive are prone to zero in on the negative. Negativity can quickly spiral until almost every word and action is met with some sort of criticism. Researchers at the Gottman Institute were able to identify what they call the "Four Horsemen of the Marriage Apocalypse."[4] These four practices—criticism, defensiveness, contempt, and stonewalling—are things to be aware of and protect against. Based on these four indicators, researchers were able to predict divorce with 90 percent accuracy.[5] What if we embraced the opposite practices? They would be encouragement, teachability, honor, and love. It turns out that God knows a thing or two about marriage. If you ever find your marriage slipping toward criticism, defensiveness, contempt, or stonewalling, seek help sooner rather than later.

Physical Intimacy

In a letter to the Corinthian church, Paul shifts to the touchy subject of physical intimacy. The people of Corinth were following the culture's cues to meet their physical desires. They were actively stepping outside the boundaries of the marriage relationship with prostitutes, mistresses, and self-gratification, among other things. Paul places all of these practices under the broad umbrella of "sexual immorality." Paul warns, "Do not deprive each other except perhaps by mutual consent and for a time, so that you may devote yourselves to prayer. Then come together again so that Satan will not tempt you because of your lack of self-control" (1 Cor. 7:5). He is offering wisdom to married couples. Rather than talk about sex, we often treat it as taboo and either hint, joke, or passive-aggressively communicate a desire for more of it or less of it.

Paul reiterates the "one flesh" concept in the preceding verses when he says that our bodies are shared in marriage, but he also emphasizes mutual consent (vv. 2–5). It's vitally important for couples to have open and honest conversations and to work together to help resist potential temptations beyond the marriage bed. For Lindsay and me, we met with an older couple and sought wisdom on this topic. The conversations that followed were so valuable for our physical intimacy. For some couples, the busyness of life may require some planning and scheduling. But even amid the busyness, be honest about your desires and work together toward possible solutions. If needed, seek counsel from a professional counselor or from older couples in your church.

Healthy Boundaries

Marriages often come under attack, and it's not always obvious where the threat is coming from. Committing to the sacred covenant of marriage means being willing to guard it. I will give you some examples that have been effective for Lindsay and me, but you and your spouse will need to decide on what works best for you. Years ago, Lindsay and I combined social media accounts because even in its infancy, social media was wreaking havoc on marriages all around us. Old friends, ex-girlfriends, classmates, and coworkers suddenly had access to our personal lives with the ability to have "harmless" communication. This has only increased with time. I don't have ongoing private conversations with women who aren't family, and Lindsay implements the same practice with men. If I need to have a one-on-one conversation (due to my role as a pastor), I let Lindsay know, or if it's an email correspondence, I blind copy (BCC) her. I give side hugs with permission, and neither of us will ride in a car alone with someone of the opposite gender.

This might all sound like a very stuffy arrangement, but it's so freeing for us! We love our marriage, and we love it enough to put barriers up for protection. One area we work extra hard to protect is our eyes. As humans, we are visual creatures, and this world is more than willing to offer pictures, videos, graphic music, and provocative marketing content. Neither of us can compete with the myriad of shapes and sizes in God's diverse creation, and neither of us should feel compelled to try. Comparison breeds dissatisfaction, and dissatisfaction breeds criticism and contempt (two of the four horsemen). The moment we said "I do" was the moment we made each other our "standard of beauty," and that standard changes as we change. I know my kids might read this, so I apologize, but I love every inch of Lindsay. And she loves all of me. The older we get, the more we change—whether for better or for worse. Learn to embrace it. Be healthy, but know that in the end, youth will give way and aging will win. Choose to love each other and avoid the comparison trap.

Marriage isn't easy but it can be a beautiful gift when done God's way. Seeking wisdom from others, verbalizing praise, serving one another, connecting emotionally and physically, and praying together are keys to a healthy and lasting marriage.

QUESTIONS FOR REFLECTION AND DISCUSSION

How is our current culture's view of marriage different from the biblical view?

What are some difficulties we face in marriage?

What are some examples of Jesus's love that we can model within marriage?

Why did God design sex to be only within the context of marriage?

What are some helpful boundaries to protect and guard your marriage?

[12]

Simple Parenting

These commandments that I give you today are to be on your hearts. Impress them on your children.

Deuteronomy 6:6–7

In this chapter, we will look at the primary directive given to parents in the Old Testament, understand the different stages of parenting, and learn how to structure our words, actions, and schedules to give our kids the best opportunity to carry on the baton of faith.

The Shema: "Hear, O Israel"

Every day, I wear two rings. On my left hand is the ring that represents Lindsay's vow to me from our wedding day. On my right hand, I wear a ring that Lindsay picked out for me in Jerusalem. Inscribed on it is the opening line of what is known as the Shema. *Shema* is Hebrew for the command "to hear." It comes from the book of Deuteronomy where God gave Moses instructions for the people of Israel to prepare them to enter into the promised land. Moses begins with the command, "Hear, O Israel: The LORD our God, the LORD is one. Love the LORD your God with all your heart and with all your soul and with all your strength" (6:4–5). In Jewish culture, you find these words written everywhere, and if possible, they are to be the last words on your lips before you die. When asked what the greatest commandment is, Jesus quotes the Shema and includes the instruction to love your neighbor as yourself (Matt. 22:34–40).

The verses that follow the Shema are instructions for parents: "These commandments that I give you today are to be on your hearts. Impress them on your children. Talk about them when you sit at home and when you walk along the road, when you lie down and when you get up. Tie them as symbols on your hands and bind them on your foreheads. Write them on the doorframes of your houses and on your gates" (Deut. 6:6–9).

We can summarize this passage to simply mean that loving God (and loving people) is not just a Sunday practice—it's the entire life of faith. God calls us to make faith a regular topic of conversation so that we can pass it on to future generations.

As parents, the most important thing we can ever do is to help our children and grandchildren know and follow Jesus. Jesus poses the question, "What good is it for someone to gain the whole world, yet forfeit their soul?" (Mark 8:36). If we give our kids the world but fail to share our faith, we've missed our calling. There are no guarantees that if we apply the principles of the Bible in our parenting, our kids will follow Jesus. After all, in the garden of Eden, you had God, the perfect parent in the perfect environment, and Adam and Eve still rebelled. However, if we intentionally parent with the goal in mind of growing faith, it will exponentially increase the chances that they will follow Jesus.

Stages of Parenting

Parents, did you know that you are the number one influence in the life of your child? At times, it may seem as though friends, entertainment, school, or culture have you beat, but studies continue to conclude that mom and dad take first place.[1] For the first quarter of their lives, you lay the foundation and set the direction of their faith. Eighteen years might feel like a long time, but the adage is true: The older they get the faster it goes. As they grow, you subtly change roles in different seasons of their lives. There are four seasons of parenting:

Caregiver

Cop

Coach

Consultant

In the early months, you're just doing your best to keep them alive and meet their basic needs of love, hygiene, and sustenance. This is the "caregiver" stage. As they begin to mobilize and experiment, you enter the "cop" phase. This stage is characterized by keeping them from danger, whether it be playing with electric sockets, wandering into harm's way, eating mystery substances, or stuffing Legos into their nostrils. The "cop" phase overlaps with the "coaching" season. They begin to step out, socialize, learn, face challenges, and walk toward adulthood. But you continue to walk alongside and direct them.

Then comes what I believe is the scariest stage. In the "consultant" phase, they are making real (potentially life-changing) decisions, hopefully with your voice echoing in their minds. It's important at this stage to not try to take over. When I meet with parents whose children are all out of the home, I ask them, "If you were to go back and parent all over again, what would you do the same and what would you do differently?" I've been surprised by how often I hear a parent say that they would have let their kids fail more often. Our tendency is to bail them out before the challenge gets real, which is a terrible way to prepare them for the realities of adulthood. Of course, there are times when we should step in. But most of the time we bail them out on things they need to experience. Instead of taking over, wait for them to come to you. After you offer your insights, it is up to them whether to follow your advice. But one thing we are called to impress upon their hearts at all times is the command to love God and people.

Words Build Worlds

Our environments are built on the words spoken within them. Another way of saying this is that our words build worlds. When you are tired or when your kid shatters your flat screen with a Spider-Man toy (true story) or when you just aren't thinking about the impact your words can have, an errant word can cause real damage. I'm guessing you can think of a time that a parent, coach, or teacher said something to you as a kid that still hurts to this day. Paul warns fathers not to exasperate (overly frustrate or enrage) their kids; instead they are to "bring them up in the training and instruction of the Lord" (Eph. 6:4). Why? Because hurt people, hurt people, and the cycle will continue for generations to come unless it is stopped.

But just as our words have the power of death and destruction, our words also have the power of life. Kids thrive when they know they are loved. And the best way for them to know they are loved is if we tell them "I love you." If these are words that are barely spoken in your home, it's time to start. If you say it a lot, it's time to say it a little bit more. Kids need to hear words of encouragement on a regular basis. It's a great way to help guide the kind of behavior we are steering them toward as adults. Do you see your kid doing things that you value? Encourage them because what gets encouraged gets repeated. Throughout the Bible and throughout history, kids have longed for blessings from their parents, and some even spend their entire lives chasing blessings that never come. One way we can help our kids succeed is by not making them chase after our blessing, but rather by offering it freely. Remind them regularly that you love them, that you are proud of them, and that you are committed to helping them succeed in life. These words are life-giving to the soul.

Of course, we won't always get our words right. But just because we used the wrong words doesn't mean they have to be the last word. One of the most powerful ways we can use words is to own our mistakes with our kids. It takes great humility, but owning up to our own messes will have a lasting impact on our kids. I believe some of my best moments as a parent have come after I have totally blown it. Our pride makes it difficult to do, but if we will genuinely apologize to our kids—when we lose our temper, push too far, forget to pick them up on time, or let a hurtful word slip out—and then ask them for forgiveness, we will model humility to our kids. We can't go back and relive our past mistakes, but we can redeem them.

More Is Caught than Taught

Words are important but more is caught than taught. Everything we do rubs off on our kids, for better or for worse. Kids don't need a list of rules and principles, they need an example they can follow, and like it or not, they will follow your example. So, begin by asking yourself, Am I modeling the kind of adult I want my kids to become? For instance, if your goal is that your kids grow up to be honest, do you tell the police officer that you know why he pulled you over? Or if your goal is that they grow up to treat their spouse with love and respect, are you investing time and energy in your marriage? Perhaps your goal is that they grow up to follow Jesus. Are you growing in your relationship with Jesus and giving room for the Holy Spirit to transform you into a different person than you were the year before? All of these practices are a far greater influence on our kids than our best intentions or motivational speeches.

Pray regularly with your kids. We pray before meals, before bed, and sometimes in the moment when we or somebody we know is facing something difficult or overwhelming. We pray with our kids, but we also pray for our kids. My most common prayer is that they would grow up to be adults who love and follow Jesus and lead their families to do the same. I'm praying that they will live out the Shema. Praying for your kids is powerful. The Holy Spirit can do things within their hearts that extend far beyond our own power. Ask Him for help. One practice my wife and I do regularly with our kids is that we read age-appropriate Bible stories with them. When they were little, it was *The Rhyme Bible*. As they got older, it was *The Jesus Storybook Bible*. As they started reading on their own, they turned to *The Action Bible*, which is styled like a graphic novel. Then they graduated to an adult Bible with an easy-to-read translation such as the New Living Translation.

One of the most important things we can model to our kids is a healthy marriage. My wife and I have a date scheduled every week with just the two of us. When our kids complain about it, as they do, I like to remind them that the greatest gift I can give them is the gift of a healthy marriage. The stronger our marriage, the more secure our kids will be. It's easy to neglect marriage for the sake of the kids, but shaky marriages will inevitably lead to shaky parenting. The reality is that our romance existed long before our kids did. One day they parachuted into this relationship and one day they will be gone, but this relationship will remain. Therefore, we want to make sure there is still something there when our kids move into the next stage of life. And when we get to that stage, we will model the kind of home we want our *grandkids* to grow up in one day.

Win the Dinner Table

As a young parent, I was taught that kids spell love T-I-M-E. There's a myth that we can replace quantities of time with some occasional quality time. That's not how it works with kids. Vacations don't replace regular absence from their lives. That is why God gave the command to impress faith *daily* on our children (Deut. 6). All the little moments add up to significant influence over time. Anne Fishel, a professor at Harvard Medical School, cites multiple studies that revealed one common practice that increases vocabulary, grades, positive mood, deep conversations, and relational quality and lowers medical risk, high-risk behavior, stress, drug use, violence, depression, and suicidal thoughts: sitting down for a meal together as a family.[2] One of the best things you can do as a parent is to share a meal each day with your kids with the television and phones turned off. Having just thirty minutes to an hour of undistracted family time around a meal adds up to thousands of hours of positive family influence in the life of a child. Win the dinner table, win the family.

Partnership with the Church

We live in a culture that celebrates busyness. We get so wrapped up in our jam-packed schedules of club sports, activities, and holidays that we end up neglecting church. Attending church is not about earning points from God; it's about experiencing the good God has for us. The benefits far outweigh the costs. There is a God-designed partnership between the family unit and the community of the church. We weren't meant to do life alone. This principle applies to our kids as well. They need community too. They need to be surrounded by other kids growing in their faith, and more importantly, they need to be surrounded by other godly adults. This is an area where the church can help by way of our kids' and student ministries.

For decades, I have worked with students, and for decades, I have seen the same story play out. It goes like this:

Parent says something to their adolescent kid.
Adolescent kid thinks their parent is stupid.
Another adult says the SAME EXACT thing as the parent.
Adolescent kid thinks the other adult is brilliant.

This is just how adolescents behave. As kids get closer to launching, they begin to wrestle with their identity. When they are younger, they want to know how they are just like their mom or dad. But as they get older, they want to know how they are different. So they begin to push away and test things out on their own. It's not because you aren't great parents but because this is just how the psychology of developing adolescents works. The greatest safety net we can put in place for this terrifying season of parenting is healthy access to the adult world in relationships with other godly adults. Maybe start by connecting your teenager to a small group at church with other students. Maybe even think about leading a small group. This can be a great way to help your kid and his or her friends process and ask questions. It takes all of us working together as one to be the church and help raise the next generation into adults who love God and love people. During the time of Jesus, the disciples tried stopping children from getting too close. But Jesus said to them, "Let the little children come to me, and do not hinder them, for the kingdom of heaven belongs to such as these" (Matt. 19:14). Children don't need to be convinced and coerced into following Jesus.

They are naturally drawn to Him. We just need to not get in their way.

Understanding how our role as parents changes in different seasons can help us prepare for how to continually lay a foundation of faith for our kids. Being intentional with our words, habits, time around the dinner table, and prioritizing church will plant seeds of faith that, Lord willing, will take root and grow for generations to come.

QUESTIONS FOR REFLECTION AND DISCUSSION

What are the principles we explored in the chapter, and how can they help you parent well?

What are positive words that have stuck with you since you were young?

What is something you can do or say to encourage a kid, grandkid, niece, nephew, or neighbor kid this week?

What is one thing you want your kids to do differently as adults than you did?

Did you grow up eating meals together as a family? Why do you think meals are so influential?

[13]

Simple Work

Whatever you do, work at it with all your heart, as working for the Lord, not for human masters, since you know
that you will receive an inheritance from the Lord as a
reward. It is the Lord Christ you are serving.

Colossians 3:23–24

We were made for work. In fact, I believe there will be life-
giving, meaningful work even after heaven and earth are redeemed. Depending on your current experience with work,
you might think working sounds like the opposite of heaven,
but that is because the work we experience on earth has been
distorted from its original design. In this chapter, we will look
at God's original design for work, understand how all kinds

of work and workers have great value, remember who it is we ultimately work for, and see work as our ministry.

God at Work

From the opening words of the Bible, we are introduced to the Creator of all things. When we are first introduced to God, He is at work. He is creating, forming, and planting (Gen. 1–2). He then invited Adam (and us) to join in the work. Adam was to care for the garden, and he was also to name all the animals. Up to this point, God had done all the naming. After He created Eve, God blessed Adam and Eve and said to them, "Be fruitful and increase in number; fill the earth and subdue it. Rule over the fish in the sea and the birds in the sky and over every living creature that moves on the ground" (Gen. 1:28). To put it another way, God could have continued forming people from the dust of the earth, but instead He gave that job to us. He could have continued creating order out of chaos, but instead He gave the order to subdue the earth to us. He could have ruled over His creation, but instead He entrusted it to us. Humans were tasked with the procreation, civilization, and rule of the earth. This was all prior to our rebellion, when everything was still "very good," which means work was a part of God's good design, not a consequence of the fall.

After the fall however, work became painful and difficult. After the fall, work began producing thorns and thistles, and basic needs were wrought with blood, sweat, and tears. It is no coincidence that Jesus wore a crown made of thorns on the cross. Thorns are reminders of the consequences of our rebellion, and Jesus wore those consequences on our behalf. It is a picture of Jesus undoing what sin has done, which means our work is not in vain. The story of redemption has begun, and a day of work without toil is coming. Our work is a small part of the greater work of God in the world to bring order out of chaos.

All Work Is Valuable

I was sitting at a coffee shop with a friend early one morning when we heard an explosion. It wasn't a gunshot or a backfiring car; this was something much more powerful. The sound caused both us and the window we were sitting by to shake. I looked around for a billow of smoke and any sign or reaction from people but saw nothing. We continued our conversation for a few minutes until *BOOM!* Another huge explosion! Still no sign of where it came from. Across the parking lot, there was a guy who appeared to be spraying weeds near a water retention area. He looked around before—*BOOM!*—the ground lifted in front of him. Curiosity compelled us to walk over and strike up a conversation with this gentleman. We learned that he had been hired by the retail complex to do pest control. A recent gopher invasion had destroyed the landscaping, so they brought in a man with a particular set of skills. He would fill the holes with a gas mixture that seeped deep into the tunnels. Once they were ignited, the resulting explosion gave off a soul-shaking boom. I left that day pondering to myself, *A gopher exploder is a job.* How many jobs exist that we are completely unaware of?

My brother is a commander with the local police department. Recently, I was in a conversation with him and the chief of police, and his chief asked, "What do you think would happen if suddenly there were no police? How long before chaos would erupt?" If every 911 call got a busy signal, I estimate it would be about fifteen minutes before we'd start seeing some smoke rising. This can be applied to so many areas. What if garbage collection stopped or the power was turned off or hospitals shut their doors or farms stopped producing or cars stopped being repaired or if everyone suddenly stopped working? There would be chaos—the very thing we are commanded to order.

All around us, there are jobs, systems, structures, businesses, and services that make civilization function, but we are so used to them that we can easily take them for granted. Everything we do is supported by a system of interwoven work spanning generations. Take something as simple as making an apple pie, for instance. First, head to the store for the ingredients. How will we arrive there? In a car? On a bike? On a paved road? Okay, let's just say we're able to walk to the store. Then, who grew the apples? How were they harvested and shipped? Where was the cinnamon grown? Who milked the cow, pasteurized the milk, and made the butter? Who mined and refined the metal for the tin? Don't even begin to think about all the work that went into the creation of the oven and the harnessing and delivering of gas or electricity. For thousands of years, systems and structures have been developing, generation after generation, layer upon layer, into the fabric of our everyday lives. For those who work in the home, there is not a job on the planet that would happen without them. We would die in one generation without those who work to create the most vital environment in creation: the home. Their work is also sacred, ordered first in the Genesis mandate to be fruitful and increase in number. All work is sacred work, continuing the work that God began in Genesis.

All Workers Are Valuable

Throughout the Bible, quality work is honored and laziness is condemned. The New Testament letters were written in a working culture that didn't have employer and employee relationships; it had masters and slaves who were viewed as property. Some people try to soften this harsh reality by noting that those who fulfilled their obligations as slaves could and often would voluntarily continue their service in exchange for a place to live and wages. But even this type of work devalued their humanity and was a direct assault on God's design. Some estimate as many as one-third of the population of the Roman Empire were considered bondservants or slaves.[1]

The Bible, however, does not promote this practice but instead teaches equality among all peoples, genders, and statuses as one in Christ Jesus (Gal. 3:28). As both slaves and masters came to faith in Jesus, they were confronted with teachings asserting the equality of all people as members of the body of Christ, the abolishment of worldly ranking systems, and the directive for followers of Jesus to regard others as greater than themselves. This raised the question of how these existing arrangements were to function going forward. God commanded them to mutually submit to one another with love and respect, a concept that had previously been inconceivable. We all have the same identity: infinitely valuable image bearers of God. Some of us may have a higher position than others, possess more talent, earn higher pay, and be more celebrated by people, but with God, there is no favoritism. This truth changes the way we see people at work along with the way we see ourselves. Our identity is not based on our work; our identity is rooted in the love of Jesus and our relationship with

Him. One day, somebody else will have your job. Does that mean you will no longer be you? Of course not. You are a child of the King, and that identity doesn't change with your job title.

A key aspect of the Christian view of work is to never connect a person's value with a person's position. If we look down on people in certain jobs or roles, it is time for a metamorphosis of thinking. The value of something is determined by the price somebody is willing to pay for it. God Himself was willing to pay with His life for every human being we ever lock eyes with. He ascribed value to every human in creation and reiterated it on the cross. To miss this is to miss the core teaching of the gospel. We have been made valuable by God, which means we are to show honor and respect to everyone in the workplace, whether they rank above or below us in the worldly structures. Even if people aren't aware of God's divine mandate, they are fulfilling sacred work in subduing the earth. There is no room in the biblical paradigm for disrespecting workers or God's work in the world.

Working for an Audience of One

Paul writes to those who were slaves or bondservants in the church:

> Slaves, obey your earthly masters with respect and fear, and with sincerity of heart, just as you would obey Christ. Obey them not only to win their favor when their eye is on you, but as slaves of Christ, doing the will of God from your heart. Serve wholeheartedly, as if you were serving the Lord, not people, because you know that the Lord will reward each one for whatever good they do, whether they are slave or free. (Eph. 6:5–8)

Paul teaches that they are to work not for their masters, but for their Master. They are to treat their earthly masters (emphasizing current reality and not ultimate reality) with respect but to embrace their new identity as one not owned by another person but owned by Christ. Paul continues, "And masters, treat your slaves in the same way. Do not threaten them, since you know that he who is both their Master and yours is in heaven, and there is no favoritism with him" (v. 9). Paul commands the earthly masters to treat slaves with the same honor and respect and to reframe their identity as well, not as a master of another human being but a fellow servant of Christ. This was revolutionary and countercultural to the original hearers.

Work Is Ministry

There is a misconception that to work in ministry you need to work for a church or nonprofit organization. While not every follower of Jesus is a pastor, every follower of Jesus is a minister according to the Bible (Eph. 4:12). Welcome to the ministry! Wherever you work, even if it is a job you don't like, there will be people who desperately need the love of Jesus in their lives. All across society, in all kinds of industry, God has strategically placed His church at this exact moment to be a light to the world (more on this in chapter 17). Working for the Lord means opening yourself each day to the work within the work for which He might have placed you there. It could be showing kindness to the employee everyone reviles, asking questions and actively listening, standing up for what is ethical, or praying with somebody going through a crisis. For some people at your work, you are the closest thing to Jesus they regularly experience. That might sound scary or intimidating, but you have the very Spirit of Jesus alive within you! If you are willing to put Him in the driver's seat, to seek and look for His leading, He will minister to them through you.

As followers of Jesus, we work hard at what we do. In the words of Paul, "Whatever you do, work at it with all your heart, as working for the Lord, not for human masters" (Col. 3:23). You might have a terrible earthly boss, but that's not who you work for. You work for the Lord. To honor the Lord, we need to do our jobs well. Long before our employers existed, God gave humanity the mandate to work to bring forth civilization. And we shouldn't squander the gifts He has given us through laziness and halfhearted effort. We are to wholeheartedly engage in whatever our job is now. If that is difficult for you to do where you work, seek another job, but continue to wholeheartedly serve the Lord wherever you are in the meantime. Don't just work for a paycheck, work to contribute something to the world. God sees your effort and will reward your work in time. Paul continues, "since you know that you will receive an inheritance from the Lord as a reward. It is the Lord Christ you are serving" (v. 24). So whatever you do, do it well.

Understanding God's original design for work helps us frame our current reality within the greater story of ultimate reality. One day, the world will be restored as it was meant to be, and work will be absent of toil. Until then, we don't fall into the trap of ranking people by position, working halfheartedly, or seeing our work as meaningless. God has called us to minister in the workplace as part of a great tapestry of workers fulfilling God's divine mandate to subdue the earth and multiply.

QUESTIONS FOR REFLECTION AND DISCUSSION

How does your job align with the divine mandate from the book of Genesis?

How can you minister to people through your current work?

What does excellence look like in your current role?

How can working hard be an act of worship toward God?

How can the principles we discussed change the way you think of work?

[14]

Simple Freedom

Be kind and compassionate to one another, forgiving
each other, just as in Christ God forgave you.

Ephesians 4:32

Following Jesus is full of actions and reactions that feel counterintuitive. The practice of forgiveness is at the top of the list.
In this chapter, we will look at Jesus's teaching on forgiveness,
understand the "why" behind forgiveness, and take practical
steps to forgive those who have wronged us. As with many
things, forgiveness is quite simple, but by no means is it easy.
As we work through this chapter, let me encourage you. The
road ahead is difficult, but it will lead you to freedom if you
choose to walk it.

Hurt

In this life you will get hurt. Living in a broken world full of broken people makes this inevitable. Hurt can take various forms—physical, emotional, sexual, relational, spiritual, financial, intentional, and unintentional. The moment we experience hurt as the result of someone else's words or actions, we begin a journey that will take us to one of two possible destinations. Either it will lead us down a path of bitterness or it will lead us down a path of forgiveness. This is because whenever we are hurt, we are owed a debt. Jesus repeatedly teaches the principle of forgiveness and models it in His response to the hurt we have caused God. Listen closely to His words as He instructs us to pray: "And forgive us our debts, as we also have forgiven our debtors" (Matt. 6:12). When we follow this practice, we are literally praying, "God, the way that I forgive others is the way I want you to forgive me." My natural self, the old self, wants to hold on to the anger and the debts that are owed to me from my past hurts. The problem is those debts can never be repaid. We may try to get even with somebody, but it doesn't undo what happened to us. There is an emotional element involved in hurt that cannot be compensated for through apologies, promises, or financial restitution. An apology doesn't erase an experience. To some degree, there will always be an outstanding debt. There will always be something owed that cannot be paid. When we hold on to the anger, it begins to take root in the form of bitterness. Bitterness is like drinking poison and hoping the other person dies; it only destroys us.

I was sexually abused as a kid. Over time, the hurt from that experience became anger, and the anger became bitterness. I not only had outward hatred toward the offender; I also had inward hatred in the form of shame. Just when I thought I had moved forward, I often found myself thinking about it, imagining revenge, and feeling sick all over again. Each time I relived the pain, the anger would grow a little more than the previous time. What angered me most of all was the thought that they had forgotten about it and that what was still hurting me wasn't affecting them one bit. Bitterness began to poison my soul. Each time I relived the event, I brought the pain of my past into the present. And all the while, I reinforced the idea that people aren't safe and that it is better to build walls for protection. Relationships require risk, and a soul poisoned with bitterness is unwilling and, in some ways, unable to open itself to risk. The deeper the relationship, the greater the risk of being hurt. Why? Because the more we open ourselves up, the more potential there is for hurt. If I am still hurting from my past, why would I ever risk anything in the present? The easiest answer is to keep everyone at a "safe" distance, which is yet another way for the hurt from the past to hurt in the present. Jesus teaches us a different way.

Jesus's Teaching on Forgiveness

Peter, one of Jesus's disciples, was wrestling with this very topic and asked Jesus this question: "Lord, how many times shall I forgive my brother or sister who sins against me? Up to seven times?" (Matt. 18:21). At the time, many of the religious teachers had concluded that forgiveness is the optimal path, but that it had limitations. Like the modern adage "Three strikes and you're out," the religious teachers taught that you should forgive someone who wronged you up to three times, but anything beyond that gave you permission to shift to anger, vengeance, and bitterness. Peter, catching on to the theme of grace and forgiveness taught and modeled by Jesus, wagered a new number. Clearly, it must be higher, so what if we double it plus one for a holier number like seven? Jesus's response was shocking: "I tell you, not seven times, but seventy-seven times" (v. 22). Our English translation doesn't do justice to the original Greek. When Jesus says "seventy-seven," a better translation would be "seventy times seven" or "seventy units of seven." I'll spare you the math: Jesus says we should forgive 490 times. The point was not that we should keep count and stop forgiving at the 491st offense, but that we shouldn't even count to begin with. How can such a way be possible? Wouldn't that mean we are just human doormats? Jesus then explains this command by way of a parable, a simple story that illustrates a profound point.

I would summarize the story in my own words, but it's impossible to improve on the simplicity and brilliance of the words of Jesus. Jesus illustrates the logic of unlimited forgiveness:

> Therefore, the kingdom of heaven is like a king who wanted to settle accounts with his servants. As he began the settlement, a man who owed him ten thousand bags of gold was brought to him. Since he was not able to pay, the master ordered that he and his wife and his children and all that he had be sold to repay the debt.
>
> At this the servant fell on his knees before him. "Be patient with me," he begged, "and I will pay back everything." The servant's master took pity on him, canceled the debt and let him go.
>
> But when that servant went out, he found one of his fellow servants who owed him a hundred silver coins. He grabbed

him and began to choke him. "Pay back what you owe me!" he demanded.

His fellow servant fell to his knees and begged him, "Be patient with me, and I will pay it back.'"

But he refused. Instead, he went off and had the man thrown into prison until he could pay the debt. When the other servants saw what had happened, they were outraged and went and told their master everything that had happened.

Then the master called the servant in. "You wicked servant," he said, "I canceled all that debt of yours because you begged me to. Shouldn't you have had mercy on your fellow servant just as I had on you?" In anger his master handed him over to the jailers to be tortured, until he should pay back all he owed. (vv. 23–34)

Forgiveness in Terms of "Debt"

Jesus takes this complex topic of hurt, anger, bitterness, and forgiveness and puts it in its simplest form. When there is hurt, there is debt. The debt owed by the first servant to the king would be the equivalent of billions of dollars today. In other words, it was completely unpayable. The penalty was that his life and the lives of his family members would no longer be their own. When the servant begs the king, the king completely forgives the debt. He doesn't demand smaller payments; he absorbs the debt and frees him. Jesus intentionally overexaggerates His point, speaking in hyperbole to shock the listener. The debt accrued by the servant is astronomical and the forgiveness given by the king is complete. Then this same servant encounters a fellow servant who owed him the equivalent of thousands of dollars today. It's no small amount until you stack it up next to the billions the first servant owed the king. We would rightfully think his response would be to pay forward just an ounce of the mercy he had been shown, but instead he does the opposite. He chooses anger and even rage at this much smaller offense by comparison. Though the fellow servant begs for mercy, he is thrown into prison.

If his response upsets you, that's because it's meant to. Through this simple illustration, Jesus gives us all a glimpse into the infinite reality of God's perspective. When the king gets word of what happened, he is shocked that his grace wouldn't ripple through the life of the servant that had been redeemed and freed. Then, Jesus poses a question for all of us: "Shouldn't you have had mercy on your fellow servant just as I had on you?" (Matt. 18:33). The answer, of course, is a resounding "Yes, of course!" Jesus is brilliant. This story is our story. Who ends up in prison in this parable? The one who refused to forgive.

What Forgiveness Is Not

Before we look at how to forgive, I believe it is important to clarify what forgiveness is not. Forgiveness is not, as we have often heard it said, "forgive and forget." Let me just tell you, forgetting is not something that comes easy to us. Memories are easily triggered (and we will talk about what to do when they are). Forgiving is not minimizing the wrong that was done with comments such as "It's no big deal." It's a very big deal! When you are hurt, the pain is real. And some hurts are even life altering. Forgiveness is not ignoring justice. If a crime has been committed, contact the police. If you have been harassed at work, notify your supervisor. If you are threatened or hurt at school, speak with a teacher, counselor, or administrator.

You can have both justice and forgiveness. They are not mutually exclusive. Lastly, forgiveness is not restoring trust. Trust is lost quickly and gained slowly. When somebody hurts you, it's your decision whether to trust them. You can choose to forgive without allowing the person forgiven the level of trust they once had. In many cases, it's wise not to offer trust to someone who has proven to be untrustworthy. If I trust you to borrow my car and you treat it like garbage, I can choose to forgive you that small offense, but there's a good chance I'm not going to entrust my car to you again.

How to Forgive

Remember Our Debt

Forgiveness is not an emotion; it's a choice. It's a conscious decision to stop sipping the poison of past hurt. How to forgive is quite simple, but again, as with many things, this doesn't mean it's easy. The steps are all woven within the parable Jesus gives. We begin the process of forgiveness by *remembering what we have been forgiven*. In the simple story Jesus shared, the king changed everything. In our story, the King changes everything. Think of the parable as if there were no gracious king in the story. It would go something like this: A guy owed another guy money. The debtor couldn't pay the guy back, so the debt collector had him thrown in prison. This sounds kind of harsh, but it's how things worked back then. The reason I struggle to forgive is that I forget about the gracious King in my own story. We hesitate when we evaluate forgiveness in light of what was done *to* us rather than what was done *for* us. In the shadow of my hurt, forgiveness feels like a decision to reward my enemy. But in the shadow of the cross, forgiveness is merely a gift from one undeserving soul to another. I have a friend who has made it a practice to go on walks and just talk with God, remembering all the wrongs my friend has committed and thanking God all over again for showing unending grace. This is the fuel for our forgiveness toward others. On the cross, Jesus declared the word *tetelestai*, which translates "it is finished" (John 19:30). It was a term used in ancient receipts to declare that a debt had been paid in full. Jesus declared our insurmountable debt of sin paid in full upon the cross. It is God's grace to us that compels us to forgive others.

Identify Their Debt

The next step is to *identify the debt*. Who is the outstanding debt with, and what do they owe us? I have indicators when I'm carrying around the hurt of a debt owed. I find myself constantly dwelling on the incident or situation. I keep an imaginary score of their offenses, replaying every foul so as not to forget. Sometimes, I clench my jaw in response, tense my body, and act annoyed by anything they say or do. Sometimes, I even get annoyed by people who remind me of them. I know I've slipped into bitterness when I start dreaming of revenge, hoping for something bad to happen to them, or getting upset when they succeed. These are all my warning signs waving the flag that I need to forgive somebody. Defining the debt is much trickier. Notice how specific Jesus was when He talked about the debt. He gave the exact number. He didn't say, "There was a guy who owed the king a bunch of money and then another guy who owed him a little to a medium bit." The king forgave a specific amount. General forgiveness doesn't free the heart of specific hurts. It wasn't until I identified what I was owed by my abuser that I was able to begin living in the freedom of forgiveness. I was owed a stolen innocence. I was owed a different childhood. I was owed a mind freed from thoughts of shame. All of these are things that cannot be paid back.

Cancel the Debt

Once identified, we then *choose to cancel the full amount of the debt.* This could be a simple decision in your heart and mind declared between you and God. It could be a more tangible act of writing it out and throwing it in a fire. Or it could even be just declaring out loud, "They don't owe me anymore." But what if they haven't apologized? What if they have already passed away? Canceling the debt is between you and God; it's not dependent on them. Your healing is your choice. In her book *Forgiving What You Can't Forget,* Lysa TerKeurst writes, "We can't change what we have experienced. But we can choose how these experiences change us."[1] It's our choice to stop sipping the poison. Jesus offers to remove the poison we have been carrying with us all of these years. We don't just trust God with our sin, we trust Him with the sin done to us. When I accept forgiveness from God, I'm set free from the penalty of my sin. When I extend forgiveness to another, I'm set free from the sin done to me. Jesus commands radical forgiveness because He loves us. We can either choose to continue to suffer the never-ending pain of bitterness poisoning us and our relationships or choose to suffer the pain of forgiving. They are both types of suffering, but one path leads to an unending prison and the other path leads to freedom. Lewis B. Smedes writes, "To forgive is to set a prisoner free and discover that the prisoner was you."[2] Bitterness has never healed anyone in the history of humankind. Only forgiveness has the power to do that. It wasn't until I could begin to pray for the good of the individual who had hurt me that I knew the poison of bitterness had been removed.

As memories are triggered and feelings follow, it's important to acknowledge the reality of the pain, to look it in the face, and to remind yourself once again that the debt has been canceled and they no longer owe you anything. Over time, this truth will begin to take root.

QUESTIONS FOR REFLECTION AND DISCUSSION

Have you ever been trapped in a cycle of growing bitterness? If so, how did you break the cycle?

What are your personal indicators that you might be carrying bitterness?

What does Jesus's parable teach us about forgiveness?

Has there ever been a time you experienced the freedom of forgiveness?

Is there anybody you need to choose to forgive today?

[15]

Simple Resolution

If it is possible, as far as it depends on you, live at peace
with everyone.

Romans 12:18

While forgiveness deals with the past, conflict resolution is
about working through conflict in the present. Conflict with
friends, family, kids, spouses, coworkers, and neighbors is inevitable in life. In this chapter, we will learn the source of every
conflict we will ever face, and then we will unpack three simple
steps to get to the other side of conflict. Working through the
steps will require humility and effort—simple doesn't mean
easy—but the end result will be a stronger relationship for
having worked through the conflict.

In 1938, Harvard began a study of their sophomore class, which happened to include future president John F. Kennedy. The study, also known as the Grant and Glueck Study, was then expanded to a second group from one of Boston's poorest neighborhoods.[1] Eighty years later and under four different directors, the study continues to seek an answer to the core question of what makes us happy and healthy in life. They amassed thousands of pages of data, meticulously gauged head sizes, conducted thorough interviews, surveyed family members, assessed net worth, extracted blood samples, and with advancements in technology, initiated brain scans and delved into genetic studies. So, what did they find? They found that relationships keep us happier and healthier. In other words, the quality of your life is determined by the quality of your relationships. Dr. Robert Waldinger, the current director of the study, shares, "When we gathered together everything we knew about them at age 50, it wasn't their middle-age cholesterol levels that predicted how they were going to grow old, it was how satisfied they were in their relationships. The people who were the most satisfied in their relationships at age 50 were the healthiest at age 80."[2] The quality of your life is not determined by income, appearance, status, athleticism, intellect, or number of followers. The quality of your life is determined by the quality of your relationships. Jesus taught these principles two thousand years ago, and a century of study and millions of dollars later, Harvard now agrees.

No Relationship Is Perfect

Jesus revealed that relationships are what matter most when He gave us the greatest commandment, which is to love God;

the second is to love people (Matt. 22:36–39). After washing His disciples' feet, Jesus qualified the kind of love we are to share: "A new command I give you: Love one another. As I have loved you, so you must love one another. By this everyone will know that you are my disciples, if you love one another" (John 13:34–35). The world will know that we are followers of Jesus by the kind of love we display to one another. But the reality is, there are no perfect people, and therefore there are no perfect relationships. God, the Author of relationships, gives us guidance on how to navigate conflict so that we can constantly maintain healthy relationships—which, as it turns out, is also good for our health and happiness.

Even still, all healthy relationships have conflict. No two people are the same, so there will be times in all relationships when there is some conflict, ranging from minor and relatively unnoticeable to major and potentially relationship-ending. It's important to remember that the quality of a relationship isn't determined by the quantity of conflicts it faces but rather by how those conflicts are effectively managed and resolved. As counterintuitive as this may sound, intimacy and deep connection are forged in the fires of conflict when handled biblically. James, the half brother of Jesus and the author of the book of James, came to faith in Jesus as his Savior after the resurrection. He puts the principles of conflict resolution into simple terms when he writes, "What causes fights and quarrels among you? Don't they come from your desires that battle within you?" (James 4:1). Every conflict is born from desires. James goes on to say that some of these desires are evil such as envy, covetousness, rage, self-centeredness, and indulgence. These desires, no matter how much we feed them, are never satisfied. We should confess and repent of all desires that fall into this category. But what about the times when desires aren't necessarily evil, just different? For example, what do we do when one person desires one thing and the other person desires another?

Toothpaste and Beyond

My relationship with my wife is the closest relationship I have. When you live close to someone for decades, you are sure to experience conflicts along the way. Early in our marriage, we had a conflict over toothpaste. There is a right way and a wrong way to squeeze the tube. I am a squeeze-from-the-bottom kind of human, using the counter edge to scrape every ounce. That is how responsible and dignified people do it. Lindsay is a middle-squeezer, too busy living her life to care about something as trivial as toothpaste. I'm slightly embarrassed to say this, but it turned into a real conflict. Both of us were shocked by the other person's perspective and immovability. I desired one thing; she desired another. Conflict. Luckily, we both agree that the toilet paper roll should tear from the front, not from the back.

When the tension of conflict arises with another person, our tendency is to say or do something as a way of communicating our displeasure. This can manifest subtly through nonverbal cues, passive-aggressiveness, sarcasm, or veiled humor. When you are on the receiving end, you pick up on the attack and immediately go into defense mode. More in line with Sun Tzu's *Art of War* than with Scripture, we launch our defense by way of counterattack. As defenses grow so do our offenses. Have you ever said something you regretted in the heat of conflict? Me too. Some of us won't fight; instead we flee, either by shutting down or even leaving. But the result is the same—a growing separation from one another. One of the ways we flee is by hashing out our conflicts with our confidants. Again, the result is a widening relational chasm. Our culture's mindset is that when the going gets tough, walk away. It's easier in the moment to change schools, find new friends, quit your job, or get divorced, but in the long run that road is far more painful and isolating than the road of healthy conflict resolution. Of course, there are times when it is wise and good to walk away from abusive relationships. However, overall, our societal tolerance for relational pain has rapidly declined, ushering in a pandemic of loneliness.

The Road to Great Relationships

Great relationships are found on the other side of conflict. Not by way of fighting or fleeing but by way of following the teaching and example of Jesus. I have seen friendships and marriages dissolve over conflict that simply needed to be worked through. What we are longing for is found through the conflict, not apart from it. James begins his treatise on relationships by saying, "Consider it pure joy, my brothers and sisters, whenever you face trials of many kinds, because you know that the testing of your faith produces perseverance. Let perseverance finish its work so that you may be mature and complete, not lacking anything" (James 1:2–4). Perseverance means that instead of giving up, sometimes we need to do some growing up, choosing the more difficult yet rewarding path. Perseverance and maturity are inseparable, and both are forged through trials. The biblical approach to conflict resolution is that rather than fighting with each other, we choose to fight for each other. There has never been a greater conflict than the one between humankind and God. Rather than fight with us, God chose to fight for us. This is who we follow. Paul tells us that in our relationships we are to adopt the same mindset as Jesus (Phil. 2:5). If we are to experience healthy relationships, we must be willing to fight for them. Combining practical wisdom and biblical guidance, there are three simple steps to resolving conflict.

Define the Problem

First, *humbly identify the conflict*. One of the common mistakes we make in a conflict is letting our emotions carry us away. It takes thirty seconds to get into a fight with someone, but fighting *for* someone takes much longer. When conflict reaches a point where it needs resolution, find a time when you aren't rushed or tired. Early in our relationship, Lindsay and I seemed to think that right as we were falling asleep was a good time to talk through something that was bothering us. You can imagine how well that went. Instead, turn off distractions such as cell phones and television so you can be fully present, and start the conversation with prayer. Ask the Holy Spirit to soften your hearts, open your ears, and help you with the relationship. I've experienced a change of heart as I was praying, before even diving into the process. As one pastor friend often says, "Jesus doesn't take sides; He takes over." If there are evil motives and desires within me regarding the conflict, I've found that when I ask, the Holy Spirit gently points them out to me.

As you begin the conversation, listen to the other person. James tells us to "be quick to listen, slow to speak and slow to become angry" (James 1:19). It's a good practice to summarize what you are hearing the person communicate back to them. I've had conflicts with people over the years that were resolved by listening and repeating back what I was hearing. I sometimes found that we agreed, but miscommunication had clouded my perception. Don't listen in order to formulate a response; first, listen to understand what the person is thinking and feeling. This is the discipline of being slow to speak as mentioned by James and echoed by Paul, who writes, "Do nothing out of selfish ambition or vain conceit. Rather, in humility value others above yourselves, not looking to your own interests but each of you to the interests of the others" (Phil. 2:3–4). Once you have listened, clarified, and repeated back, then you are ready to clearly, concisely, and kindly share your perspective and desires. Work together to define where the desires are misaligned. Once identified, you can move to the next step.

Brainstorm a Solution

Second, *work together to find a possible solution.* Now that you know what kind of conflict you are dealing with, pray for wisdom (James 1:5). If you are uncomfortable praying out loud, you can pray silently. God loves relationships. He created them for us, and He created us for them. I believe God wants to walk with us through the conflict. As you begin to brainstorm, remember that you are working together as a team. This is not the time to criticize each other or each other's ideas. There are no bad ideas. Everything is on the table. This is the principle of mutually submitting to one another "out of reverence for Christ" that Paul writes about to the Ephesian church (Eph. 5:21).

Lindsay and I were on vacation one time, and weeks of unresolved conflict bubbled up in paradise. We were miserable.

Having taught these principles to dozens of young couples, we knew the power of working through these steps. We sat on the bed and first identified our misaligned desires. Then, with hotel stationery in hand, we began to brainstorm ways to either meet in the middle or try something completely outside the box. Some of the suggestions were terrible—mostly from me—but she kindly wrote them down until we got to the bottom of the page. We started crossing off the least reasonable ideas first until we settled on one to try.

When you take the approach of working together, shoulder to shoulder, to resolve a conflict, you go from viewing the problem as being between you to instead viewing the problem in front of you together. Rather than conflict being a barrier, it becomes a unifier. Like soldiers in the trenches, fighting for each other builds a deeper connection.

Evaluate

Finally, *run the experiment and evaluate its effectiveness.* You are now relational scientists, hypothesizing and running experiments. The potential solution may not be the final answer. Every relationship is different because every person is different. What works for one conflict or person might not work for another. My wife and I rescued our marriage by buying our own tubes of toothpaste. She is free to destroy hers all she wants.

Set a time to follow up on your conflict resolution and honestly evaluate its effectiveness. Celebrate and encourage progress, not perfection. Small steps over time make a big difference in long-term relationships at home, at work, and with neighbors and friends. Thomas Edison was asked about the long, arduous process of harnessing electricity after continuous failed attempts. Edison said, "I have not failed. I've just found 10,000 ways that won't work."[3] If the experiment fails, celebrate that you now know another way not to resolve the conflict. Run the process again and try something different. If you get stuck along the way, ask for help. Life's too short and relationships are too important to allow conflict to sabotage them.

Conflict is unavoidable at times, but resolution is a choice. Choosing to resolve conflict rather than discard relationships will build deeper intimacy and a healthier life. Working together to clearly identify conflict, brainstorm possible solutions, and run the experiment will draw you closer in your relationships, even if the experiment doesn't work out at first. Persevere as Christ persevered for us, and share in the joy of restored relationships.

QUESTIONS FOR REFLECTION AND DISCUSSION

What are the three steps of conflict resolution, and how will you apply them into your daily life?

Have you ever grown closer to someone through conflict?

Is your natural tendency to react to conflict with a "fight" response or a "flight" response?

Is there somebody you need to set aside time with to resolve a conflict?

Why do you think that today's culture is more prone to run away from relationships than previous generations? Do you think that is healthy or that the pendulum has swung too far?

[16]

Simple Power

The tongue has the power of life and death, and those who love it will eat its fruit.

Proverbs 18:21

We have touched briefly on the power of our words in previous chapters, but it is worth taking a deeper dive on this subject. In this chapter, we will look at what the Bible says about how to use the power of our words for building up others and a biblical case study of how one individual used their words to change history for the good.

Creation began not by the power of work but by the power of words. God spoke light into existence. When God created human beings in His image, He created us with the ability to speak words. He entrusted to us a similar power to create or, when used improperly, to destroy. It was with the power of words that Satan called into question the goodness of God, tempting Eve and Adam into what would be the destruction of our world. Words build worlds both literally and figuratively. Our relationships are primarily built on the words we speak to one another. The environments of our homes are not built by the furnishings and decor but by the words spoken within the walls. Throughout history, words have declared war and words have brought peace. Every great movement of humanity has been built on words.

Slow to Speak

James devotes much of his treatise on relationships to the topic of words. In the first chapter of the book of James, he pours out great wisdom with one simple command: "Be quick to listen, slow to speak and slow to become angry" (v. 19). Have you ever said something you immediately regretted? Early in our marriage, my wife and I were just wrapping up college. We knew how to snack, eat fast food, and say yes to dinner invites. Neither of us knew how to cook. Once we built a budget, we knew we would need to grocery shop and cook meals at home. It was difficult at first. Lindsay looked up a recipe for spaghetti and went to work. We sat down together, prayed, and took our first bites. She asked me, "So what do you think?" I would like to take a moment for all the guys reading this. If you are ever asked, "So what do you think?" I encourage you to pause, even if only for a second, and think to yourself, *What are they really asking?* I did not. Instead, I told her what I thought: "My mom's is better." I can still hear her fork dropping on the plate.

I learned a valuable lesson that day, a lesson that I could have learned the easy way had I paid attention to the teachings of James. We must learn to hit pause before we unleash the power of life and death from our lips.

So much conflict could be avoided if we learned to pause, think, and then speak. Instead, we opt for the fire, ready, aim approach. There's great wisdom in learning to hit pause. James warns against my profession (pastor) when he says, "Not many of you should become teachers, my fellow believers, because you know that we who teach will be judged more strictly" (3:1). I, along with all who teach, will be held accountable for our words. And we won't always get them right. James goes on to say that anyone who never faults with their words would be in the category of perfection (v. 2). He equates the tongue to the bit placed in a horse's mouth, the rudder on a ship, and the spark that starts a fire. It's something so small and yet so powerful. James comments that "all kinds of animals, birds, reptiles and sea creatures are being tamed and have been tamed by mankind, but no human being can tame the tongue. It is a restless evil, full of deadly poison" (vv. 7–8). Can you see the picture he is painting? Our words are powerful beyond measure. Destructive words (boasting, criticism, gossip, slander, lies, and anger) can leave a wake of scorched earth in our relationships. Solomon in his great wisdom writes, "Sin is not ended by multiplying words, but the prudent hold their tongues" (Prov. 10:19). There is power in the pause.

Words That Wound

When I was a sophomore in high school, I sensed God calling me to pastoral ministry. At a camp for students, there was a breakout session for those who sensed this call. Out of hundreds of students attending the camp, there were about twenty of us who attended the session. The session was led by an older gentleman who had pastored for decades. He asked us why we wanted to be pastors and pointed to me first. Caught off guard, I responded sheepishly, "My life has been greatly impacted by my youth pastors, and I want to do the same for others." He pointed to me and addressed the room, "You see, that is not a calling to ministry." I was crushed. His words haunted me for years. Even reliving them now whispers to my struggle with impostor syndrome (feeling unworthy).

Nowhere greater have I seen the moldable power of words than when spoken into the lives of kids and students. Just as my own story is marked by moments of discouragement, the opposite is also true. I had more than one youth pastor, volunteer, parent, teacher, coach, aunt, uncle, and grandparent encourage me along the way. I've seen a child's countenance completely change by a positive word spoken to them. Kids and students need regular affirmation that they are seen, known, loved, and supported. Generations have passed where children rarely heard the words "I'm proud of you" from a parent—a blessing longed for in every family. In the Old Testament, Jacob and Esau fought for their father's blessing, something Jacob would again wrestle over later in his life but with God. No matter how much the world will encourage the wrong things in our lives, our ears are specially tuned to the voices of significant adults.

Paul writes to the Ephesians, "Do not let any unwholesome talk come out of your mouths, but only what is helpful for building others up according to their needs, that it may benefit those who listen" (Eph. 4:29). The first part of this instruction can only happen after we learn to pause before we speak. Before we unleash our words, we must pause and weigh the potential damage they may cause. I receive a lot of great encouragement, for which I am truly grateful. However, I still receive criticisms. And as much as I try not to let them, the criticisms stick with me far longer and pierce me far deeper than the encouragements. A mentor of mine once said, "I can receive one hundred letters, ninety-nine of them encouragements, one of them a criticism. So, what do I do? I throw away the ninety-nine and memorize the one." He uses this to illustrate the destructive power of negative words. No matter how much we fight it, harsh words still sting. If you are unsure of your words, it's better to wait a little longer and, if needed, come back to the conversation. Ask yourself, Do these words destroy, or do they build up? In the words of Thumper quoting his parents, "If you don't have somethin' nice to say, don't say nuthin' at all."[1] We live in an age where criticism reigns. Comments written online, while not spoken directly from the tongue, still carry the fire of hell with them. If we would apply the simple principle of using helpful words that build up, the world would be a different place.

Words Worth Speaking

In his letter to the Philippians, the apostle Paul gives a list of things for us to think on in lieu of anxious thoughts. He writes, "Finally, brothers and sisters, whatever is true, whatever is noble, whatever is right, whatever is pure, whatever is lovely, whatever is admirable—if anything is excellent or praiseworthy—think about such things" (4:8). I would add for us to speak about such things. The more we marinate our minds on the goodness of God and the truth of His Word, the more our internal metamorphosis will be evidenced externally. Jesus said that the words we speak are an overflow of what is in our hearts (Matt. 12:34). If our words are destructive, the answer is not for us to simply hold our tongues; we need to examine our hearts. What we allow into our hearts and minds will ultimately seep out through our words. As the old saying goes, "Garbage in, garbage out." The alternative must be true as well: "Goodness in, goodness out."

Power of Encouragement

Throughout this book, we have often quoted from Paul's letters to the churches God used him to help start across the Roman Empire through missionary journeys. Those journeys, subsequent letters, Mark's Gospel, and the launch of the Gentile church would not have happened the way they did if it weren't for the powerful words of one behind-the-scenes individual named Barnabas. His real name was Joseph, but the apostles (the original disciples of Jesus) gave him the name Barnabas, which means "son of encouragement" (Acts 4:36). Barnabas looked for the positive in people, and he often spoke it to them and to others. Paul had a dark past of persecuting the church before coming to faith in Jesus, so when he came to faith, the apostles in Jerusalem rightfully had their doubts. Paul had his hand in arresting, beating, and even killing their friends. But Barnabas stood up for Paul. He used his influence to vouch for Paul's genuine faith in following Jesus (9:27). When Gentiles started coming to faith and being filled with the Holy Spirit, the church in Jerusalem questioned it, even sending Barnabas to investigate. When he saw what God was doing, he encouraged the church to keep spreading the good news of Jesus.

In Acts 11 and 15, Barnabas brought back the news that the gospel was for everybody, no matter their background.

Barnabas traveled with Paul on their missionary journeys around the Roman Empire, and as Paul grew in leadership, Barnabas humbly stepped into a supporting role. When Paul wanted to return to the churches they helped establish, he wanted to leave John Mark behind because he had deserted them when things grew dangerous on a prior trip. Despite Paul's own second chance, he was unwilling to take the risk with Mark. Barnabas stood up for Mark, and together he and Mark continued as missionaries while Paul went with Silas (Acts 15:36–40). At the end of his life and ministry, in the shadow of imminent death, Paul writes his second letter to a young pastor named Timothy. At the close of this letter, he implores Timothy, "Get Mark and bring him with you, because he is helpful to me in my ministry" (2 Tim. 4:11). Throughout his life, Barnabas used his influence and words to build up and encourage others, and God used those words to shape the New Testament and the early church.

The Perfect Ratio

In an attempt to find the perfect ratio of encouragement needed to thrive, the *Harvard Business Review* noted a study that found top performing business teams operate in an environment where there are 5.6 positive statements for every one negative.[2] The Gottman Institute for Marriage found that among the healthiest couples, the ratio is 5 to 1.[3] This does not happen by accident. It happens when we intentionally choose to speak words that build others up. Truett Cathy once asked, "How do you know someone needs encouragement? If they're breathing." If a person has breath in their lungs, then that is the international sign that they are in need of encouragement. You never know what God might do through a simple word of encouragement. I met a woman in our church whose life had been radically transformed by the love of Jesus. With tears in her eyes, she shared with me the story of how she ended up at our church. She was working as a waitress and going through an exceptionally difficult season, when two couples who were eating at the restaurant took time to encourage her and were even given the opportunity to pray for her. They invited her to come to our church and then left a generous tip before leaving. She came that weekend, heard the good news of God's grace, and said yes to following Jesus. What might seem like an ordinary moment on an ordinary day might be a divine opportunity to speak the power of life into an individual who is inwardly dying. You possess that power.

You wield the power of life and death with your words. Give life to those around you. Build up those who look up to you by pausing before you speak and by offering them the gift of encouragement. The quality of your relationships will be a direct reflection of the quality of words spoken within them.

QUESTIONS FOR REFLECTION AND DISCUSSION

What does the Bible say about the power of words?

Who has been an encourager in your life?

Have you ever said something and immediately wished you had paused first?

Are there any careless words spoken to you as a child that still stick with you today?

What are some practical ways you can encourage others?

[17]

Simple Light

You are the light of the world. A town built on a hill cannot be hidden.

Matthew 5:14

I was afraid of the dark when I was little. Gifted with a wild imagination (as most kids are), I could fill in the unknown with some pretty terrifying things. All I needed was the smallest nightlight or my door slightly cracked open to dispel the darkness and, along with it, my deepest fears. The nature of darkness is that it doesn't exist. It's not a thing; it's the absence of a thing. Darkness is simply the absence of light. For those who live in spiritual darkness, it can be terrifying. In this chapter, we will discuss how we can be light wherever God has placed us through hospitality, welcoming outsiders, listening, and pursuing those who are still in the dark.

The Light of the World

Jesus said, "I am the light of the world. Whoever follows me will never walk in darkness, but will have the light of life" (John 8:12). Those who follow Jesus are freed from spiritual darkness and are entrusted with the light. In the Sermon on the Mount, Jesus looked at His followers and instead of saying "*I* am the light" He told them, "*You* are the light of the world. A town built on a hill cannot be hidden" (Matt. 5:14). This picture was significant for Jesus's hearers. In the ancient world, cities were synonymous with safety. If a person was on the road after sundown, they were vulnerable to wild animals, bandits, or the elements. Cities were strategically located on the tops of hills, fortified with walls and gates for protection. They cut through the darkness and showed the way to safety by way of torches, lamps, and candles.

When Jesus calls us "the light of the world," He is emphasizing our calling to show the world the way to safety, the way to salvation, the way to Him. After the resurrection, Jesus appeared to hundreds of His disciples for days before gathering with the core eleven (the twelve minus Judas). Matthew records, "Then Jesus came to them and said, 'All authority in heaven and on earth has been given to me. Therefore go and make disciples of all nations, baptizing them in the name of the Father and of the Son and of the Holy Spirit, and teaching them to obey everything I have commanded you. And surely I am with you always, to the very end of the age'" (Matt. 28:18–20). This is known as the "Great Commission." The greatest commandment and the Great Commission are two sides of the same coin because there is no greater act of love than to introduce someone to Jesus. Notice that the emphasis of the Great Commission is on the word "them." Who is "them"? Anybody and everybody from all nations who doesn't yet know and follow Jesus.

Be a Light Where You Live

Where you live right now is not random. Wherever you live, the light of the gospel shines. Inviting people into our homes is an invitation into the light. We don't just open our homes to those we already know; we invite people we have just met in our neighborhoods, for example, to share a meal together. My wife is amazing at engaging with people from all different backgrounds. She has a gift for loving people. My wife, along with another outgoing neighbor, has created a culture of community in our neighborhood—something increasingly challenging in the age of pulling into a garage and closing the door. Together they organize community holiday celebrations with potlucks in the park. Foods from across the world make these some of my favorite meals. On the first Monday of every month, there's an open invitation to all women to bring a chair and a drink to a designated driveway where they can get to know one another.

Hospitality

One of the opportunities we have to be a light to others is through what the Bible refers to as "hospitality." The Greek word for hospitality literally means "love for strangers."

Hospitality is the opening of our homes and our lives to others, sharing meals and listening to one another's stories. As implied in the word, hospitality is about turning a space into a spiritual hospital where people can experience healing.

Years ago, our church started doing something known as Alpha. I was first introduced to Alpha outside an old Anglican church in London on a cold and rainy January evening. I remember looking at a line of people wrapped around the church and down the street, hundreds of individuals who were waiting to get in, the majority of whom were self-declared atheists, agnostics, or unaffiliated with any faith. How was it possible that in London (a very post-Christian city), hundreds were waiting in the rain to get into a church while the pubs were open? God was doing something here through the power of hospitality.

I learned later that there was a lot going on behind the scenes prior to this event. Many people were involved in hours of prayer, intentional friendships, and courageous invitations, all of which demonstrated a posture of unwavering hospitality. Those who entered the church found a judgment-free zone. All were welcomed and offered a warm meal. People all over the room were engaged in conversations, intentional about getting to know each guest. There was a short presentation consisting of somebody's story, thoughts about life's biggest questions, and varied opinions from all over the world. Then, gathered in small groups across the room, the guests were invited to discuss what they thought about what they just heard. No idea was criticized. No questions were foolish. And the amazing thing was, the hosts didn't correct crazy responses or even provide answers. They just asked questions and listened. The vast majority of those who continued the course came to faith in Jesus by its end. Since experiencing Alpha, we have made it a regular practice at our church. Groups often meet in homes where the gift of hospitality is best expressed.

One example of hospitality in the Old Testament is when Abraham goes out of his way to care for three strangers who turn out to be angels from the Lord (Gen. 18). In reference to this well-known account, the author of Hebrews writes, "Do not forget to show hospitality to strangers, for by so doing some people have shown hospitality to angels without knowing it" (13:2). We take this same posture as we gather as a church and welcome those who are strangers. Many people make up their minds about church within the first few minutes of being inside the church building. The kindness of strangers goes a long way when somebody is trying something for the first time. A greeting, a smile, holding the door, or an invitation to somebody to sit with you can go a long way.

Gentleness and Respect

In the book of 1 Peter (a letter addressed to the followers of Jesus scattered across the Roman Empire by persecution), the apostle reiterates the greatest commandment and the Great Commission. He says we are to love God (1:8), love others (1:22), and make disciples (2:9, 12). Peter writes, "Always be prepared to give an answer to everyone who asks you to give the reason for the hope that you have. But do this with gentleness and respect" (3:15). We should be prepared to share why our hope is in Jesus, but we do this in a way that is loving.

I was with a friend who was in town for the weekend, and we headed downtown to share a meal together. It was a Friday evening, and the area was brimming with people. As we walked out, I could hear the garbled sound of a mega-phone and almost immediately knew what it was. My heart sank. Somebody was shouting at passersby that they were going to hell. Families had to speed up their steps to not have their eardrums blasted with what came across as the furthest thing from love. What was sad was that some of what this person was saying was true, but they had wrapped it in a package that nobody—including me—wanted to receive. In his letter, Peter emphasized the need to share our hope with gentleness and respect. Jesus, as John writes, came "full of grace and truth" (John 1:14). Truth without grace is just plain obnoxious (1 Cor. 13:1–3). But to withhold truth, even though it might be taken as offensive, isn't loving. If a child is wandering into traffic and somebody pulls them back, it is a great act of love, though to the child it may seem offensive at first. This is the tension we are to live in alongside Jesus. We are to be full of grace and full of truth, to be bold and gentle at the same time.

To Listen Is to Love

Jesus set an example for His disciples (and for us) when He washed their feet before a meal. He said that by following His example we would experience blessing (John 13:1–17). At the time, the washing of feet was a common practice of hospitality for those entering a home for a meal. Coated with the dust and debris of walking along unpaved roads, feet washing served a basic need and was often done by those of the lowest social rank. Today, I believe one of the greatest basic needs is to be known and heard. Listening is like a modern-day version of the washing of feet. To listen is to love.

A friend once taught me a simple tool for conversation when meeting someone new. It follows the acrostic FORM, which stands for **F**amily, **O**ccupation, **R**ecreation, and **M**otivation. People love to talk about these four topics, and by showing genuine interest in others, we take on the ancient posture of bending down with a water basin and a towel. For family, perhaps ask them about their siblings. If they are a parent, ask them about their kids. I could talk to you for hours about my children. For occupation, simply ask, "What do you do for work?" Learn about their job, why they chose it, what they love about it, or if it's their long-term career plan. For recreation, ask them, "What do you do for fun?" When they have free time, how do they prefer to use it? Motivation is a little bit of a deeper topic. Maybe you can start with, "What are your hopes and dreams?" Is it retirement, starting a nonprofit, volunteering, traveling the world? These questions serve as the first step toward getting to know someone. Resist the urge to dominate the conversation and, instead, take the posture of a learner. The Great Commission begins with the greatest commandment: to love God and others. And to listen to others is to love others.

The Heart of a Father

I had a dream shortly after we had our first son, Gabriel. It was one of those dreams that is so vivid you think it might be real. In the dream, I was caring for Gabriel as we were running errands, and suddenly I realized he was no longer with me. I traced my steps back, asking if anyone knew where my son was. I knocked on doors, growing more frantic as I picked up my pace. I found myself entering a large gathering hall in a church full of familiar faces. They welcomed me warmly and were happy I was there. I asked them about my son, and they ignored the desperation in my voice. They continued being friendly, but what I needed was for them to care. I raised my voice and said, "Do you not understand that I have lost my son!?" I began to shout over the mingling of the crowd, "Will anybody please help me find him! I don't know if he's safe, I don't know if somebody has him, if he's hurt, all I know is that he's lost, and I need to find him!" I woke up afraid and angry, my heart racing. It took me a moment to realize I was dreaming. I did what parents do in these moments and walked into Gabriel's room and stared at him asleep in his crib. As I watched the slight movement of his chest as those tiny lungs filled with air and let it out, my own breathing began to match his, and I started to feel my heart calm. As I headed back to bed, I prayed a simple prayer in reference to the dream: "God, what was that?" The Holy Spirit whispered back to me, "That is how I feel every single day." The Great Commission is of the greatest importance to God. He loves people more than anything else, and so many are lost whether they know it or not. The greatest act of love is to introduce somebody to Jesus.

We are not here by accident. Jesus calls us the light of the world and commissioned us to help show the way to safety by creating hospitals of hospitality, welcoming outsiders, loving through listening, and seeking those who are lost.

QUESTIONS FOR REFLECTION AND DISCUSSION

What does it mean to be "the light of the world"?

What would it look like for you to be a light on a hill where you currently live?

How does the Bible describe hospitality?

Who is somebody that you can show love to through active listening?

Jesus washed His disciples' feet the day before His death. What are some things we can do for others to serve them?

[18]

Simple Story

> But you will receive power when the Holy Spirit comes on you; and you will be my witnesses in Jerusalem, and in all Judea and Samaria, and to the ends of the earth.
>
> Acts 1:8

There are many notable last words in recent history. Leonard Nimoy, best known for his role as Spock in *Star Trek*, posted, "A life is like a garden. Perfect moments can be had, but not preserved, except in memory. LLAP"[1] (which stood for his catchphrase "live long and prosper"). Reggae star Bob Marley told his son, "Money can't buy life."[2] Winston Churchill, who was always memorable with his words, said, "I'm bored with it all" before slipping into a coma.[3] Steve Jobs, the multibillionaire cofounder of Apple, uttered the words, "Oh wow. Oh wow. Oh wow."[4] What makes the words of Jesus different from famous last words of notables in history is that Jesus wasn't on His deathbed. He was standing, victorious over death, proven by the resurrection. His final words weren't ponderings or reflections. His words were orders—orders to unleash the news that what was once dead could be made alive again. In this chapter we will learn how to share this news with the power of our story.

Witnesses, Not Salespeople

Acts 1:8 records the final words of Jesus before His ascension into heaven. After His ascension, the disciples went into Jerusalem where they awaited the promised arrival of the Holy Spirit. On the day of the Spirit's arrival, the church was born and so began an era that continues today. As each new follower of Jesus receives the gift of the Holy Spirit, they are empowered to bear witness to others.

Where we make a mistake as followers of Jesus is that we often see ourselves as salespeople. Jesus didn't say we would be salespeople or saviors. We are to be *witnesses*. A witness is someone who tells others what they have seen or experienced. Early in my faith, I thought it was my job to convince everybody to follow Jesus. This is not entirely wrong. In fact, the defense of the Christian faith is something I have spent much of my life studying. This area of study, known as apologetics, stems from the Greek word *apologia*, meaning "to give a defense." Apologetics isn't a bad thing; I strongly recommended it for those wrestling with their own skepticism. The only challenge is, Jesus didn't give us orders to play defense. The church has been "given the ball," so to speak, which means we are on offense. And as Jesus Himself said, He will build His church, and the gates of hell will not overcome it (Matt. 16:18).

While it's good to know the reasons for the hope that we have in Jesus, Jesus does not pressure us to be able to debate every academic atheist or angry agnostic. We are not on a mission to argue against every false belief. We are called to proclaim the truth of Jesus and His work in our lives to the world. When I was younger, my grandmother taught me that when federal detectives were trained to spot counterfeit currency, they didn't start by observing the wide variety of fakes. Instead, they were taught to recognize the real thing. They learned all there was to know about the currency and security measures so that when a fake came across their desk, they could immediately recognize it as such. Rather than spend all our time learning to debate every countless argument, we're invited to get to know Jesus by spending time in His Word, listening to the whispers of the Holy Spirit, and in the godly wisdom of others.

The Power of Story

Speaking of apologetics, if anybody had the ability to debate somebody into faith, it was the apostle Paul. Much of what has been referenced in this book comes from his writings. Paul was brilliant. He was an expert in the Old Testament, a Roman citizen by birth, an eloquent communicator, and a gifted and highly influential leader. Paul is considered by many to be the most influential person in the history of the church. So, what was his strategy? Did he dismantle the inconsistencies of polytheism, deliver all the evidence of the resurrection, point out their inherent sinfulness, or share the hundreds of prophecies foreshadowing and predicting Jesus as the Messiah? He did not. He shared his story. Paul, who was notorious for persecuting the church, encountered the resurrected Jesus on the road to Damascus, and his life was forever transformed when he received the Holy Spirit.

As Paul grew in influence and boldness, he shared his story with all who would listen. One time in Jerusalem, Paul was arrested and about to be killed when the Roman commander interrupted the uproar. There, standing in front of a massive crowd, Paul was given an opportunity to speak. Knowing this could very likely be his final words, Paul shared his story (Acts 21:27–22:21). Later, Paul faced multiple trials until eventually he faced King Agrippa. When given the opportunity to address the king, what argument did Paul use? Once again, he told his story (Acts 26:2–23). Agrippa responds, "'Do you think that in such a short time you can persuade me to be a Christian?' Paul replied, 'Short time or long—I pray to God that not only you but all who are listening to me today may become what I am, except for these chains'" (Acts 26:28–29). I love his response and the sincerity with which he expressed it. Paul had experienced something nobody, not even a king, could take away from him, and he wanted everyone else to experience it too. Throughout his letters, Paul continued to lead with his story.

In the book of John, we read a story about a man who, for his entire life, knew only darkness. He was born blind, forced to sit near the temple steps in Jerusalem and be dependent on the generosity of sojourners and worshipers who would occasionally toss him a coin. He could only imagine what the holy temple must have looked like by way of the audible gasps of onlookers as they passed by and their voices faded into the distance.

One day, he hears the tumult of a crowd moving toward him. When it stops in his vicinity, he hears them talking about his condition, turning his struggle into a theological discussion. The crowd is directing their questions at a man who declares Himself the light of the world with a prefix reserved only for God Himself. He draws close and holds the blind man's face, something only his parents had ever done. He rubs something over the man's eyes and sends him down to the pool of Siloam to wash. This is no short trip. As the blind man descends the ancient steps over a third of a mile, he most likely can make out the psalms of ascent sung by those approaching the holy ground. Upon washing, he blinks, and for the first time the light of the world rushes in. Joy and tears fill his eyes as he ascends back up the steps, singing the songs by heart that he has heard his entire life.

All of Jerusalem took notice. Every trip to the holy places, they had seen this man. Although they did not know him, they all knew of him. The change was evident. This was the man they had grown so familiar with, but at the same time, he was now a completely different person. For the first time, he must have heard silence from the crowd with their mouths hanging open while he alone was the one singing. Because this took place on the Sabbath, the religious leaders (who were already plotting to kill Jesus), recognized this as breaking their man-made rules. They confronted the man, wanting to debate the theology behind the healing. Unable to engage in their argument, he fell back on what he was most certain of: "One thing I do know. I was blind but now I see!" (John 9:25).

There is power in a story. People can argue and debate many things, but it's difficult to debate the power of a changed life.

Every week I hear a story of a changed life. It's probably my favorite part of my job. I've met former addicts, prostitutes, gang members, womanizers, atheists, and outwardly successful yet inwardly miserable individuals—all sharing the commonality of lives unrecognizable compared to their past. It wasn't a well-laid argument that changed them. What changed them was the overwhelming love and grace of Jesus Christ saturating their lives by His Spirit. And there truly is no debating that fact. It's the most powerful evidence that Jesus is alive and that the Holy Spirit is at work in the world. He's still in the business of changing lives, and He can and will change yours and the lives of those you love if you will let Him.

Your Story

One of the most powerful tools you possess to shine the light of Jesus on the world is your story. While some stories may have similarities, every story is unique. If you've never shared your story, you may not know where to begin. I recommend using the simple formula we saw in the stories of the apostle Paul and the man who was born blind. It follows the same structure that divides history, which we separate into two parts with a line in the middle. Whether we use the abbreviations BC (before Christ) and AD (short for the Latin phrase *anno Domini*, "in the year of our Lord"), or we use BCE (before the Common Era) and CE (Common Era), the line is the same: the birth of Jesus. Jesus is also the line that divides your story.

Your Life Before Jesus

Your life before Jesus is the first part of your story. For Paul, the first part of his story was that he was a persecutor of the

175

church, zealous for religion, and committed to shutting down what he thought was heretical teaching. What was your life like before you met Jesus? Do you remember what it was like to live without knowing Him and His love? What were your priorities? What was the condition of your heart? Was there a longing for something more? Sometimes I will talk with those who came to faith at an early age. Some have expressed embarrassment that they don't have a better or more compelling BC story. If that is you, praise Jesus that He rescued you at such a young age! One exercise I like to do for my own life and that I recommend to others who came to faith young is to ask yourself, How would my life look different today if I had never met Jesus? This can be a scary question to ponder, but it is eye-opening as to all that Jesus has rescued you from. All of this can be included in the BC portion of your story.

The Line in the Middle: The Moment You Came to Faith

How did you first meet Jesus? Did you grow up in a household of faith? Did somebody invite you to church? Did you have a rock-bottom moment that caused you to turn to Jesus? Was it similar to Jacob, wrestling with God? Perhaps somebody shared their story of how Jesus changed their life and invited you into a relationship with God. The Holy Spirit loves to draw people to Jesus in a variety of different ways. I've met those who experienced some miracle in their life after a follower of Jesus prayed for them. I've met people from places where following Jesus is forbidden. They came to faith through recurring dreams and visions. I know of a man who tried taking his own life. After he cried out to God, someone knocked on his door and introduced him to Jesus. For Paul, it was encountering the resurrected Jesus on the road to Damascus. These are all great love stories of a God who goes to great lengths to reconcile us to Himself. The Holy Spirit is constantly at work in the world, drawing hearts back to God. I was introduced to Jesus through my family and church. As a young child, I was in the category of people Jesus addressed when He instructed, "Let the little children come to me, and do not hinder them, for the kingdom of heaven belongs to such as these" (Matt. 19:14). That was my story, and it is no less powerful than any other story of God rescuing a soul destined for destruction and bringing that soul from death to eternal life.

How Jesus Has Changed Your Life

The second part of your story, the change that Jesus has brought, is sprinkled with hope. It is the AD of your calendar—your life since meeting Jesus. The apostle Paul made a complete turnaround after meeting Jesus, going from the chief persecutor of the church to being the chief persecuted for the church and to a life dedicated to the sharing of the gospel. How has Jesus changed your life? How have your relationships changed? What is your time with the Holy Spirit like? What transformation have you already seen happening from the inside out? How has your thinking changed? Do you see people differently? Do you see yourself differently?

One invisible but palpable change is that you have been made spiritually alive in Christ and have been filled with the Holy Spirit, who is a seal of your adoption and a deposit guaranteeing your inheritance (Eph. 1:13–14), and who testifies to your spirit that you can call the all-powerful Creator God "*Abba*, Father" (Rom. 8:15). For me, I was no longer who the world said I was—what I had done or what had been done to me. I had been made new. I became a child of God and have experienced firsthand the overwhelming love He has for me, which compels me to share Him with others. What I know for certain—for me and for you—is that we are far from perfect. We are all on a journey of transformation that will continue throughout our lifetimes. But we, along with those in the early church and all who have followed since, remain "confident of this, that he who began a good work in [us] will carry it on to completion until the day of Christ Jesus" (Phil. 1:6).

The Sacred Symbol of Baptism

One of the ways we share our story is through the symbolic picture of baptism. This ancient practice was modeled by Jesus and has been commanded to those who would follow Him. Baptism is a word that means "to immerse under." If you've never seen a baptism, it's simple yet powerful. It can take place in any body of water. In ancient Israel, they had ritual baths called mikvehs that were often used. The person performing the baptism must be someone who is a follower of Jesus, often a pastor but not required. Baptism begins with a declaration or affirmation of faith in Jesus by the person being baptized. I always ask the person if they have put their faith in Jesus as their Savior and leader and choose to follow Him all their days. Then I say, "I baptize you in the name of the Father, the Son, and the Holy Spirit," following the instruction that Jesus gives to us in the Great Commission. The person is dunked under the water and then lifted back up. At my church, we like to celebrate when they come out of the water because Jesus said there is great rejoicing in heaven when someone turns to faith (Luke 15:7), and we want to join the party.

Baptism is a picture of what occurs in our lives. Standing in the water represents our BC. Going under the water represents that our old life is dead and gone. As we come out of the water, we enter our AD, our new life of faith in Jesus and partakers in His resurrection. Paul writes it this way to the church in Galatia: "I have been crucified with Christ and I no longer live, but Christ lives in me. The life I now live in the body, I live by faith in the Son of God, who loved me and gave himself for me" (Gal. 2:20).

Every follower of Jesus has a story with the power to inspire faith in others. As witnesses of the work of Jesus in our lives, we offer hope to those in search of more. Using the framework of BC, the moment we came to faith, and AD, we have a simple formula used by the greatest evangelists to continue the spread of good news throughout the world.

QUESTIONS FOR REFLECTION AND DISCUSSION

Why did Paul use his own story when he was speaking in public?

Is there anything that hinders your confidence in sharing your faith with others?

What is your story? How can you share your story with others?

Who is somebody you can share your faith story with this week? Who is somebody you want to ask to share their story with you?

What is baptism and why do you think Jesus commands this as one of our first steps of faith?

Conclusion

Simple Hope

And I heard a loud voice from the throne saying, "Look! God's dwelling place is now among the people, and he will dwell with them. They will be his people, and God himself will be with them and be their God. 'He will wipe every tear from their eyes. There will be no more death' or mourning or crying or pain, for the old order of things has passed away."

Revelation 21:3–4

Our faith is driven by hope in the promises of God. His promises are good, and His promises are true. As we have walked this journey of understanding the reliable foundations of our faith and taking intentional steps to apply our faith to our everyday habits and relationships, my prayer is that you have already experienced the intersection between your faith and God's faithfulness. God often meets us in areas of life only accessed through simple steps of faith. While some of those steps may seem small, the compounding effect of faithfulness over a long period of time will take you further than you could ever ask or imagine (Eph. 3:20). Exercising our faith is a lifelong practice that will culminate with the day our faith becomes sight. Paul writes, "For now we see only a reflection as in a mirror; then we shall see face-to-face. Now I know in part; then I shall know fully, even as I am fully known" (1 Cor. 13:12). We confidently wait for that moment when faith becomes sight.

In the final pages of *The Lord of the Rings*, after the dark shadow has lifted and the sun is shining, Samwise Gamgee asks Gandalf a question: "Gandalf! I thought you were dead! But then I thought I was dead myself. Is everything sad going to come untrue?"[1] This picture painted by J. R. R. Tolkien is of the promise that lies ahead for all followers of Jesus. Tim Keller expanded upon this thought when he wrote, "Everything sad is going to come untrue and it will somehow be *greater* for having once been broken and lost."[2] In other words, if anything is not good, it is simply because God is not yet done. The darkness we experience in this life will one day be lifted.

John, the last remaining of the original disciples of Jesus, died in exile on the island of Patmos. On that island, he received a revelation of things to come at the end of this age, recorded as the last book of the Bible known as "Revelation." Filled with symbolic imagery, Revelation tells us how the story will end. But the Bible is not a beginning, middle, end kind of story. It is a beginning, middle, *new beginning* story. Jesus will return and ultimately defeat Satan, sin, sorrow, and death. All evil will be wiped out for all time, and we will experience the eternal life for which we were created, freed from the penalty, power, and even presence of sin. We will forever be in the presence of God, basking in His eternal light. Until then, we continue forward in simple steps of faith. Faith is "confidence in what we hope for and assurance about what we do not see" (Heb. 11:1).

Take confidence that your steps of faith are never in vain. They are the beginning steps of an endless journey that we walk with God. May you daily experience the blessing of simple faith.

Acknowledgments

The journey of writing *Simply Following Jesus* was not walked alone. I am grateful for the countless individuals who have poured into my life over the years and modeled the practices laid out in this book. I thought about writing out all the names, but it would put me over my contracted word count. If you are thinking "maybe that includes me," it does. Thank you!

Lindsay, you have shown me what real love looks like despite my flaws. I am honored to walk the path of faith with you until Jesus calls us home.

Gabriel, Corban, and Emma, thank you for your patience as you often found me working on the manuscript in the backyard with noise-canceling headphones and a computer. You are already great models of faith, and I pray you will continue to pass the baton of faith to future generations.

Chad, you are brilliant at taking deep truths and communicating them in their simplest form. Much of this book reflects our decades of ministry together.

Sun Valley, thank you for not just going to church but for being the church and changing the world around you. Every week I am inspired by the stories of simple faith in action.

Debbie, thank you for getting this book started, and Eddie, thank you for the hours of work to make it coherent. Baker Books, thanks for believing in this project to help more people follow Jesus and experience the abundant life that follows.

Notes

Introduction

1. Alice Calaprice, ed., *The Ultimate Quotable Einstein* (Princeton University Press, 2010), 202.

Chapter 2 Simple King

1. Wayne Grudem, *Systematic Theology: An Introduction to Biblical Doctrine* (Zondervan, 1994), 226.

Chapter 4 Simple Prayer

1. Anne Lamott, *Help, Thanks, Wow: The Three Essential Prayers* (Riverhead Books, 2012).
2. Madhuleena Roy Chowdhury, "The Neuroscience of Gratitude and Effects on the Brain," PositivePsychology, April 9, 2019, https://positive psychology.com/neuroscience-of-gratitude/.
3. "Anxiety Disorders—Facts & Statistics," ADAA, accessed May 8, 2024, https://adaa.org/understanding-anxiety/facts-statistics.

Chapter 5 Simple Transformation: Lies

1. Julie Miller, "A History of Woody Allen and Soon-Yi Previn Describing Their Relationship, from 'The Heart Wants What It Wants' to 'I Was Paternal,'" *Salon*, July 30, 2015, https://www.salon.com/2015/07/30/a_his tory_of_woody_allen_and_soon_yi_previn_describing_their_relationship _from_the_heart_wants_what_it_wants_to_i_was_paternal/.
2. Rick Warren, *The Purpose Driven Life* (Zondervan, 2002), 19.

Chapter 6 Simple Transformation: Truth

1. Brother Lawrence, *The Practice of the Presence of God*, trans. John Delaney (Image Books, 1977), 15.

Chapter 8 Simple Finances

1. Summer Allen, "The Science of Generosity," Greater Good Science Center, May 2018, https://ggsc.berkeley.edu/images/uploads/GGSC-JTF _White_Paper-Generosity-FINAL.pdf.
2. Matthew 5:23–24; 5:26; 5:42; 6:1–4; 6:19–24; 6:25–34; 7:9–12.
3. "World GDP per Capita 1960–2024," MacroTrends, accessed May 8, 2024, https://www.macrotrends.net/global-metrics/countries/WLD/world /gdp-per-capita.
4. Ron Chernow, *Titan: The Life of John D. Rockefeller, Sr.* (Random House, 1998), 66.

Chapter 9 Simple Rhythms

1. C. S. Lewis, *Mere Christianity* (HarperOne, 2001), 154.
2. Quoted in Ryan Buxton, "What Seventh-day Adventists Get Right That Lengthens Their Life Expectancy," HuffPost, July 31, 2014, https://www .huffpost.com/entry/seventh-day-adventists-life-expectancy_n_5638098.
3. John Ortberg, *The Life You've Always Wanted: Spiritual Disciplines for Ordinary People* (Zondervan, 2002), 76.
4. John Pencavel, "The Productivity of Working Hours," IZA, April 2014, https://docs.iza.org/dp8129.pdf.
5. Dietrich Bonhoeffer, *Life Together: The Classic Exploration of Christian Community*, trans. John W. Doberstein (HarperOne, 2009), 99.

Chapter 10 Simple Worship

1. A. W. Pink, *Exposition of the Gospel of John* (Baker Books, 1975), 208.
2. Nayantara Dutta, "Why We Remember Music and Forget Everything Else," *Time*, April 14, 2022, https://time.com/6167197/psychology-behind -remembering-music/.
3. Lucy Notarantonio, "How the Viral 'Red Car Theory' Could Change Your Life," *Newsweek*, January 13, 2024, https://www.newsweek.com/red -car-theory-viral-tiktok-1859159.
4. Richard Foster, *Celebration of Discipline: The Path to Spiritual Growth* (HarperOne, 1978).
5. Warren, *The Purpose Driven Life*, 98.

Chapter 11 Simple Marriage

1. Christy Bieber, "Revealing Divorce Statistics in 2024," *Forbes*, January 8, 2024, https://www.forbes.com/advisor/legal/divorce/divorce-statistics/.

2. Tyler J. VanderWeele, "Religion and Health: A Synthesis," in *Spirituality and Religion within the Culture of Medicine: From Evidence to Practice*, ed. J. R. Peteet and M. J. Balboni (Oxford University Press, 2017), 173–75.

3. Brad Wilcox, "Faith and Marriage: Better Together?," *Institute for Family Studies* (blog), July 6, 2017, https://ifstudies.org/blog/faith-and-marriage-better-together.

4. John M. Gottman and Julie S. Gottman, "Gottman Couple Therapy," in *Clinical Handbook of Couple Therapy*, 5th edition, ed. Alan S. Gurman, Jay L. Lebow, and Douglas K. Snyder (Guilford Press, 2015), 129–57.

5. Sybil Carrere and John M. Gottman, "Predicting Divorce among Newlyweds from the First Three Minutes of a Marital Conflict Discussion," *Family Process* 38, no. 3 (1999): 293–301.

Chapter 12 Simple Parenting

1. See Urie Bronfenbrenner, *The Ecology of Human Development: Experiments by Nature and Design* (Harvard University Press, 1979); Robert Crosnoe and Glen H. Elder Jr., "Family Dynamics, Support Systems, and Educational Resilience during Adolescence," *Journal of Family Issues* 25, no. 5 (2004): 571–602; Paula Fomby and Andrew J. Cherlin, "Family Instability and Child Well-Being," *American Sociological Review* 72, no. 2 (2007): 181–204.

2. "Benefits of Family Dinners," The Family Dinner Project, accessed May 8, 2024, https://thefamilydinnerproject.org/about-us/benefits-of-family-dinners/.

Chapter 13 Simple Work

1. See Keith Hopkins, *Conquerors and Slaves* (Harvard University Press, 1978); Keith Bradley, *Slavery and Society at Rome* (Cambridge University Press, 1994).

Chapter 14 Simple Freedom

1. Lysa TerKeurst, *Forgiving What You Can't Forget* (Thomas Nelson, 2020), 85.

2. Lewis B. Smedes, *Forgive and Forget: Healing the Hurts We Don't Deserve* (HarperOne, 2007), 59.

Chapter 15 Simple Resolution

1. "Study of Adult Development," Harvard Second Generation Study, accessed May 29, 2024, https://www.adultdevelopmentstudy.org/grantand glueckstudy.

2. Robert Waldinger, "What Makes a Good Life?," DailyGood, January 8, 2016, https://www.dailygood.org/story/1196/what-makes-a-good-life -robert-waldinger/.

3. Matthew Josephson, *Edison: A Biography* (Viking Press, 1959), 100.

Chapter 16 Simple Power

1. *Bambi*, directed by David Hand, Walt Disney Productions, 1942.

2. Jack Zenger and Joseph Folkman, "The Ideal Praise-to-Criticism Ratio," *Harvard Business Review*, March 15, 2013, https://hbr.org/2013/03 /the-ideal-praise-to-criticism.

3. Gail Golden, "The Gottman Ratio for Happy Relationships at Work," *Psychology Today*, June 29, 2022, https://www.psychologytoday.com/us /blog/curating-your-life/202206/the-gottman-ratio-happy-relationships -work.

Chapter 18 Simple Story

1. Leonard Nimoy (@TheRealNimoy), "A life is like a garden," Twitter, February 23, 2015, 2:36 a.m., https://x.com/TheRealNimoy/status/56976 2773204217857.

2. Andrew Amelinckx, "These Were Bob Marley's Tragic Final Words," Grunge, February 3, 2024, https://www.grunge.com/1508080/bob-marley -tragic-final-words/?zsource=msnsyndicated.

3. "Churchill's Last Words: 'I Am Bored with It All,'" *New York Times*, February 2, 1965, p. 12.

4. Sam Jones, "Steve Jobs's Last Words: 'Oh Wow. Oh Wow. Oh Wow,'" *The Guardian*, October 31, 2011, https://www.theguardian.com/technology /2011/oct/31/steve-jobs-last-words.

Conclusion

1. J. R. R. Tolkien, *The Return of the King*, part 3 of *The Lord of the Rings* (Houghton Mifflin, 1993), 930.

2. Timothy Keller, *The Reason for God: Belief in an Age of Skepticism* (Viking, 2008), 33.

ROBERT WATSON is the teaching pastor at Sun Valley Community Church, one of the fastest growing churches in America, with seven locations across Arizona. He speaks at camps and conferences across the country and trains communicators both locally and internationally. Robert has degrees in sociology and church leadership from Southwestern Bible College and Bethel Seminary. He and his wife, Lindsay, have three children and live in Chandler, Arizona.

Connect with Robert:

 @robertwesleywatson